INTELLIGENCE & COMPASSION
IN ACTION

The Seven Pillars for Social Entrepreneurs

To Marshall Welch

In Harmony With Hope

Lauren Speeth, MBA, DBA, DMin

Intelligence & Compassion in Action; The Seven
Pillars for Social Entrepreneurs

ISBN 978-0-9859753-0-2

Printed in USA

DEDICATION

To James Earl Carter, Jr.,
whose wisdom inspired the
writing of this book, and
to Rosalynn Carter. Their
intelligence and compassion
in action is unrivaled.

TABLE OF CONTENTS

NOTE FROM JAMES EARL "JIMMY" CARTER

39th President of the United States of America

"When Lauren Speeth asked me for advice about how to work effectively for social change, I was glad to share my experience with her. She rewards me and The Carter Center with much praise in this book. In return, I want to praise her for expanding my advice into a plan of action that is both practical and idealistic. I believe that her book can be a guide for entrepreneurs who want to make the world a better place."

– JIMMY CARTER

FOREWORD

The concept of lifting compassion from the heart where it resides and launching it into action, of using it to make a difference, shift awareness, promote change, is intriguing. Particularly if done with research and reason, with intelligence and intent, and with the mindfulness that it all began with the heart.

Likely you have read many other books with promising titles, indicating their words will show you how to pave a path toward positive change in the world. Perhaps the initial pages were inspiring, leaving you eager to make the journey. Yet you reached the last pages without a road map, a guide or a moral compass.

You may have noticed how these books generally fall into one of a few predictable categories: self-help books on how to maintain motivation for change or become more businesslike; books on assorted tactical aspects of running a nonprofit; stories about the state of the world and the few who are making an impact on it; and books about theological dogma for making a difference. Some were not applicable to your situation, and none offered everything you needed to get where you are trying to go.

This book bridges a gap, presenting established ideas in a modern methodology, inspired by the wisdom of President James Earl "Jimmy" Carter. This methodology is about mindfulness, integrating different aspects of life and work into a broader, more comprehensive context. Readers can apply what you learn to your own situations, in a positive and life-affirming approach to social entrepreneurship.

Clearly explained and practically applied, you will find it useful, whether you are developing your vision or looking for a new framework for revitalizing ongoing work.

– KENNETH TAM, EXECUTIVE DIRECTOR
THE ELFENWORKS FOUNDATION

PREFACE

Looking out my window to the worries of the world, and noticing how many ways it seemed to be crying out for help, it seemed very big and broken, and I felt very small. It was 2005, and Elfenworks had just begun its social entrepreneurial work on behalf of our country's future. Our goals were to identify issues that weren't being effectively addressed, create change in new and different ways, and amplify project successes through storytelling. But first, we needed to know how.

I was an absolute beginner. Although I held a doctorate in business administration and had deep background in computers and technology project management, I had no direct experience in the field of social entrepreneurship.

Overwhelmed, I prayed for guidance, and soon was offered a brief audience with President Jimmy Carter, whom I had never before met, but whose work I respected immensely. In a conversation that lasted no more than a few minutes, he summed up for me the key areas in which I'd need to focus, and encouraged me to follow my passion for change. I was both thrilled and encouraged.

The wisdom I gleaned from that initial conversation, now known as the "Seven Pillars," has grown over the years into the entrepreneurial methodology my team and I apply daily at Elfenworks. I was so taken with it that I decided to make it the subject of a doctoral dissertation when I went back to school, this time to study theology. I realized that, although the methodology itself was secular, it was a fitting companion to the teachings that interested me at the time. My dissertation was completed, and I graduated with a doctorate in ministry, in June of 2011.

Now, I am pleased to share with you the wisdom that informs our work.

– DR. LAUREN SPEETH

ABOUT THE AUTHOR

Dr. Lauren Speeth is the visionary force behind Elfenworks Productions, LLC, a producer of internationally acclaimed and Grammy®-nominated media content, and the founder of The Center for Non-Harming Ministries. As founding CEO of The Elfenworks Foundation, *"In Harmony with Hope®,"* she has assembled a team of social entrepreneurs of the highest caliber, with deep and far-ranging expertise in multimedia outreach, computers and technology, music, film, management, law, finance, education, human development and social justice.

Dr. Speeth has used her bridge-building skills to forge alliances with other groups, such as Campus Moviefest, encouraging students to create social justice content; Golden Gate University, in poverty law; Saint Mary's College, in Fiduciary Capitalism; Mills College, for Socially Responsible Business; and The Center on Poverty and Inequality at Stanford University, recently named a National Poverty Center and with which Elfenworks established The Collaboration for Poverty Research.

The Elfenworks team has developed a considerable library of online resources, including multilingual stress reduction visualizations for children, awards programs, awareness-raising efforts, and empowerment tools for nonprofits, socially responsible businesses and private citizens. Dr. Speeth is called upon regularly to evaluate web and film content, and she currently serves on various advisory boards, among them the Board of Regents of Saint Mary's College and the Board of Councilors of The Carter Center.

In 2010, for her commitment to poverty law, Dr. Speeth was

honored with a Doctor of Laws Honoris Causa from Golden Gate University School of Law in San Francisco, where she earned her Doctorate in Business Administration in 1992.

In addition to her DBA, Dr. Speeth also holds a Doctorate in Ministry from Bakke Graduate University in Seattle, Washington; an MBA from Saint Mary's College, and a BA in Psychology from Mills College. She has completed three distinct courses of study at Stanford: a summer internship as a chaplain at Stanford Hospital, an Advanced Computer Security Professional Credential program, and a summer program for philanthropy leaders at the Graduate School of Business. She holds lifetime Community College Teaching Credentials in three areas: finance, management and computers.

Born in New York, Speeth spent her childhood on the East Coast, the Midwest and also India, where her parents founded an experimental school for untouchables (Dalits) outside New Delhi. A self-professed "tech geek" whose extensive travels have made her a citizen of the world, Speeth has spent her life utilizing her experiences and skills to help create social change both locally and globally. With Northern California as her home base, as well as the base of operations for The Elfenworks Foundation, Dr. Speeth continues to work with a team of partners on issues surrounding inequality and its resulting suffering among humankind.

ACKNOWLEDGEMENTS

A project of this nature is never done in isolation, and this one is lifted up by the hands of many. I want to acknowledge their contributions, but in doing so, I know I will unwittingly omit many whose names are written in my heart. For that, I apologize in advance. I want to thank, first and foremost, my friends at The Carter Center, and most especially former President Jimmy Carter, for exceptional support and guidance, not just during my dissertation research and throughout this book project, but during my day-to-day work at Elfenworks as well.

I also thank everyone – faculty, staff and students – at Bakke Graduate University (BGU) Seattle, where I completed the foundational research for this book, as part of my doctoral dissertation.

I am very grateful to my editor, Lisa Crawford Watson, for helping me bring this project to fruition. I recognize the Elfenworks team, trustees, and consultants, past and present, who have given me feedback or guidance, and particularly Kenneth Tam, for the foreword; Marian Brown Sprague, for early copy editing; Mike Dalling, for the sparkle on my graphics; and Ryan Paul, for helping me puzzle out the various font idiosyncrasies in Hebrew and Greek.

I am thankful to all the social entrepreneurs I interviewed and whose work has shaped my views, as well as my personal friends, mentors, and family. Thank you for your inspiration, encouragement and patience.

Finally, thank you, readers, for caring enough about the world to continue seeking methodologies to help you be more effective in implementing your vision for change. The world's problems are in good hands with you.

INTRODUCTION

Many of us have valid, deeply heartfelt ideas about change. Yet often, we don't understand how to develop our sensibilities into an effective plan of action. Within these pages, I offer you the "Seven Pillars," a methodology designed to help you develop a deliberative mental framework for change.

Whether endeavoring to create a business model, develop project plans or fulfill life aspirations, this simple, elegant, yet empowering approach is derived from wisdom former President Jimmy Carter shared with me when I was starting out as a social entrepreneur. I sought his guidance chiefly because he has an established reputation as someone who identifies a social problem and uses compassionate yet entrepreneurial principles – particularly risk and initiative – to create the venture that will mitigate or solve the problem.

A lot of business books separate the fundamental elements of business from the conceptual, as is often the practice in business school. Yet in life, they all must operate cooperatively, simultaneously and in sync. Applying the Seven Pillars methodology enables entrepreneurs to integrate all the disciplines of business into a whole-life scenario, creating a comprehensive way of thinking about your world and the work you do, no matter what your field and no matter what your theological perspective. For some, this might be considered more of a "life coach" than entrepreneurial methodology. Certainly, while I use many examples of social entrepreneurs, whose vision for success includes meeting the world's needs, this methodology could work for anyone seeking to make a difference.

The Seven Pillars is a methodology presented without the use of religious language or denominational ties, yet I do feel it works best when the practitioner is grounded in a strong wisdom or faith

8

tradition. For that reason, at the end I will introduce supplementary readings that address some of the faith traditions and discuss with you how they can create a context to help motivate social action.

HOW I RECEIVED THIS WISDOM

When I became a social entrepreneur, concerned with seeking innovative solutions to society's pressing social problems, I often felt overwhelmed by the enormity of it all. I didn't know where to begin or how to jump in and help. Although I was well educated from a practical standpoint – I held a master's degree and a doctorate in business – I had never been taught how to think about visionary social entrepreneurship.

Without a plan of action, my thoughts of just showing up and rolling up my sleeves didn't seem very useful. I didn't want to exhaust myself without making a difference. At the same time, I realized other people were being effective, and I longed to understand how. As I prayed for guidance, my prayers were answered in 2006 when I was granted a private audience with former President Jimmy Carter.

Photograph by John Moores, Sr.

FIRST MEETING WITH PRESIDENT JIMMY CARTER

I told President Carter I was new to the work of social change in which he had such experience, and I presented him with my most pressing questions. "Mr. President," I said, "How do you choose among all your possible projects? How do you not get discouraged or overwhelmed? How do you make a difference?" He responded by telling me about the seven criteria[1] he would suggest I use to guide my work. I knew I would never forget his response, and I was eager to apply it:

1. Keep to your vision despite corrosive naysayers.
2. Bring your special skills to bear.
3. Fill a chasm where you are truly needed.
4. Cultivate partnerships.
5. Readily share the credit.
6. Have a valid feedback loop to understand your impact and allow for course corrections
7. Take a long-term view, allowing for bumps on the way.

I sensed, as I heard his words, how satisfying they were, and I realized his criteria could become the tools that would enable me to lay the groundwork on which to build my path toward change. It hasn't been an easy road, yet it has been a truly joyful journey. And now that I have built from that wisdom, a set of pillars to frame my route, and I have made sense of the valuable experience gained along the way, I am ready to take others with me.

---

1   Jimmy Carter, conversation. Private audience with Lauren Speeth, San Francisco, CA, January 13, 2006.

ILLUSTRATION: THE SEVEN PILLARS

DOES THIS METHODOLOGY WORK?

In a word, yes! Particularly if we understand what we mean by "work." Does it help us to get where we're going? Does it enable us to be agents of change? Not only have I used and taught the Seven Pillar methodology successfully over the years, I have used it to analyze other organizations, including The Carter Center. I also have used it at The Elfenworks Foundation, including as a way to judge other social entrepreneurs in the selection process for our annual *In Harmony with Hope*ˢᵐ awards, which recognize those groups and individuals working to mitigate the problem of poverty in America. Many of these awardees have since shared their thoughts with me about the methodology.

One question I often hear is, "As opposed to what?" People wonder if there is some other framework worth considering. Of all the entrepreneurs I interviewed during my research, none had an alternative mental construct to offer me. So, my answer is, it works better to think within a structured framework, than to work without any formal scaffold. The methodology doesn't stand in opposition to, nor does it replace, other aspects of business, such as accounting, finance, public relations, fundraising, marketing and so on. Instead, it creates the structural integrity from which these other entrepreneurial elements can operate.

This advice isn't relevant to entrepreneurs seeking a "get rich, quick" scheme. Far from it. There are easier paths to getting rich, certainly quicker than trying to save the planet or interceding on behalf of others. But I am convinced there is no quicker path to joy. I have found deep satisfaction in following my heart to meet the world's needs. For those of you intent on such a path, this book promises to be an empowering tool; a compass or a roadmap, guiding you along the way toward your destination.

WHO CAN BENEFIT FROM THE SEVEN PILLARS?

Virtually anyone who cares about others – students, young activists, recent graduates, executives, CEOs, doctors, lawyers, dentists, mothers, grandparents, or retirees – can use this methodology to become a more effective change agent. The CEO of a high-tech database company sets out to solve the problem of identity theft among children in foster care. A dentist wishes to set up a free monthly clinic for preventive cleanings. A pastor endeavors to empower his or her congregants to assist in uplifting and healing themselves and others. A business school professor teaches ethical entrepreneurship, socially responsible business, or fiduciary capitalism to help prepare students to make change. A middle- or high-school teacher whose goal is to inspire students as change-makers begins teaching this rubric to students by adding it to the curriculum, accompanied by case studies to help them apply it. Anyone with an idea and heartfelt intentions should feel empowered by this methodology.

IS THIS METHODOLOGY SECULAR OR RELIGIOUS?

One reason the Seven Pillars is so effective is because it is practical rather than merely theological in nature. The wisdom that lies at the basis of the methodology came from a former president, who is a practicing Christian. Yet it is easily generalized, without a religious language or framework. Practitioners of any faith tradition, or those who have a true interest in social entrepreneurship for purely humanitarian reasons, can find it of value. No one needs to be excluded from using it on ideological grounds.

Admittedly, as the author, I cannot escape my own beliefs and biases. I believe good works are most effectively implemented when grounded in a faith practice of some kind, and many faith traditions support and encourage positive "heal the world" attitudes and actions. The first of the Seven Pillars invites broad vision or inspiration, which requires staying the course or keeping the faith. I truly believe we all do better when we feel support, inspiration and guidance from a higher power, however we might refer to that power. This is true for social entrepreneurs, who often try what others would presume impossible: to change the world for the better.

Because of my faith orientation, in a set of essays at the end of this book, I discuss those traditions with which I am familiar: Judaism, Buddhism, Islam and Christianity; exploring what they have to say in support of empowered action. If your tradition is not included here, please don't feel excluded; I just don't feel qualified to go further. Although I delve most deeply into Christianity, the Pillars are ideal for use by a broad spiritual base among entrepreneurs. Whatever your faith tradition, consider the wisdom of these pages in light of the teachings you know, and apply it to your work.

INTENT OF THIS BOOK

This is a book about how to think about social action, what

it means to be a social entrepreneur, and how perspective and intention guide such action. All of this effort is undertaken to empower the social entrepreneur for the advancement of the greater good. The intent of this book is to facilitate the success of new generations of social entrepreneurs in two ways. By linking the Seven Pillar methodology to fundamental teachings, it makes a case for millennia-old methodologies as a framework for the social entrepreneur. And, by creating a useful instrument, it is action-oriented. Whether the social entrepreneur is working on social justice, peace, environmental or other issues, all of humanity stands to benefit from an empowered leader – someone prepared to guide rather than control.

Empowerment reduces the cognitive dissonance that arises out of an inability to envision solutions; when solutions can be imagined and realized, it is no longer necessary to turn a "blind" eye to problems that previously seemed overwhelming. If we find ourselves able to see only what we believe is possible to solve, this methodology may help us look past our unintentional social blindness to envision social change.

The Seven Pillar practice is particularly useful to people interested in making a difference yet lack a rubric for moving forward in an effective and thoughtful way. I am convinced of this because I have seen it in action at The Carter Center, and I have put it into action at The Elfenworks Foundation. This Seven Pillar methodology is empowering, enabling regular people to make an exceptional difference. This is good news for those who do not believe their situation is hopeless yet seem to lack a framework for change.

As a storyteller, I believe the presence of an empowering model, combined with a compelling internal narrative, can encourage an individual to challenge society's norms without experiencing dissonance. It is my deepest intention that through this book I am providing a practical, working methodology to help create an alternative personal storyline that can turn apathy into action, and willful blindness into clear vision. For those who feel caught between apathy and despair, this text offers a third option: empowered action.

CHAPTER QUESTIONS

1. *How do you define "social entrepreneur"? Do you agree with this concept of empowerment? Do you believe change is possible without this mentality?*

2. *What are the Seven Pillars? Can you imagine how they can be used as a framework for social change?*

3. *Describe a case of social blindness. Consider how you, as a social entrepreneur, might go about opening eyes to the change you have envisioned.*

4. *How do you feel about convening historically religious doctrine and contemporary wisdom on social entrepreneurship? Are there dangers? If so, what?*

CHAPTER 1 - SOCIAL ENTREPRENEURSHIP, PAST AND PRESENT

A BRIEF HISTORY

The term social entrepreneurship is of relatively recent coinage, yet social entrepreneurs have existed since commerce began. For centuries, the only avenues available to social entrepreneurs were within the confines of church or state – not in society. The early social entrepreneurs – the Jesuits, Benedictines, Franciscans and Lasallians – tested the boundaries of those systems, and out of their challenges grew today's establishment. Today, social entrepreneurs are found within social, political, religious, spiritual, nonprofit/ foundation, hybrid, and for-profit constructs, and they are still pushing the boundaries.

A social entrepreneur of historical import was St. Francis of Assisi. The Italian Catholic friar relinquished what could have been a path of luxury, choosing instead a life of service that embraced poverty. He rebelled against his father, against the power elite, and against the moneyed classes. Rather than be ruled by his father, he shed his father's clothing and left his father's home, stark naked. The church father, seeing his purity of heart, clothed him in his own robe, and allowed him to go forth with his blessing, to rebuild the local chapel, following God's call.[2]

Similarly, St. Bernard of Clairvaux was a noble youth who restored the Rule of St. Benedict. A guide for monastic life, the French abbot typified by rhythm, measure, service, and dedication

---

2   George Ferguson, *Signs and Symbols in Christian Art*, (London, England: Oxford University Press, 1961), 119.

to God.[3] Consider also, St. Ignatius of Loyola, who developed month-long "spiritual exercises" as a path to awakening a deep personal relationship with Jesus Christ, and who founded the Jesuits.[4] St. Thérèse of Lisieux developed an approach to spiritual life that people of every background can understand and adopt.[5] St. Jean Baptiste de la Salle formed the Christian Brothers and taught the poor youths of France so well that the French nobility sent their children to his schools.[6] All were social entrepreneurs.

Had the term social entrepreneur been coined, likely none of these people would have considered themselves as such. Yet that's what they all were. More recently, the inventive solutions of Saint Damien of Hawaii enabled him to act as healer, builder, teacher, and general caretaker. He gave his life to care for people with leprosy on the island of Molokai, and was canonized in 2009.[7]

Another entrepreneur, a revolutionary in the field of medicine, was Florence Nightingale, an English nurse whose work influences the way hospitals are designed and built today. When nursing was not yet considered a respectable profession for young women of stature, she made it so. A stickler for detail and measurement, she took great pride in her charts and graphs, and presented them as gifts. Ms. Nightingale is said to have lowered the death rate from 43 percent in British Army hospitals to two percent between February and March 1855. She revolutionized nursing by applying a rather progressive understanding that today would seem a matter of common sense. As David Bornstein, author of *How to Change the*

---

3   Ibid., 108.

4   Saint Ignatius of Loyola, *Personal Writings*, (New York, NY: Penguin Classics, 2004).

5   Day, Dorothy. *Selected Writings*, (Maryknoll, NY: Orbis Books, 2007), 187-203.

6   Luke Salm, FSC., *The Work Is Yours; The Life of Saint John Baptist de La Salle*, (Landover, MD: Christian Brothers Publications, 1996).

7   Anwi Skinses Law and Richard A. Wisniewski, Kalaupapa, *National Historic Park and the Legacy of Father Damien, A Pictorial History* (Honolulu: Pacific Basin Enterprises, 2007, with stapled updated insert, 2010), 71.

World: Social Entrepreneurs and the Power of New Ideas, points out, "The existence of knowledge and the widespread application of knowledge are very different things."[8] It was quite some time before Ms. Nightingale's practices became widespread.

With industrialization, greater world travel, the elevation of the middle class, a new order of elites with a social conscience, and generally longer life spans, new opportunities arose at the turn of the last century to make a positive difference.

A century later, global media has linked the world in ways never before imagined, and the social entrepreneurs began to mobilize with yet another level of empowerment.

Oprah Winfrey established a leadership academy for girls in South Africa. Bill and Melinda Gates created their foundation to extend innovations in health, development, and learning to the global community. Yet it does not always begin with money. Bill Milliken drew on his personal history of alienation from high-school to found Communities In Schools, the nation's leading community-based organization helping kids stay in school and prepare for life. Jenn Adams established the Maisha Project to provide clean water and improve the wellbeing of children and their families in Tanzania. They started their organizations armed with little more than an idea and heart.

Beginning with the recession of 2008, a rising tide of poverty has ignited social conscience and action by some, while forcing others, now just trying to get by, to reduce their giving. Many nonprofits shut down in the wake of the economic downturn; others consolidated. Corporations latched on to trendy terms such as *green, social value creation, or multiple bottom lines* as a way to

---

8   David Bornstein. *How to Change the World: Social Entrepreneurs and the Power of New Ideas.* Updated Ed. (New York, NY: Oxford University Press, 2007), 44.

sell themselves to a more conscious market.[9] It is sometimes hard to walk the fine line between real commitment to sustainable practice and what has become known as "green washing" the proverbial fence. What is the agenda, and is it sincere? It is against this backdrop that I present a new methodology for change.

SOCIAL ENTREPRENEURS NEEDED NOW

It is time to alter the way we operate. I consider it important and possible to be both rational and systematic in making a transformational difference on large-scale problems. Because change is desperately needed, positive visionary agents need to become empowered with practical wisdom that will work in a contemporary context.

I believe the lack of a clear roadmap for making lasting, positive, measurable change in unknown territory is leading to frustration and less-than-optimal attempts at making change. This perceived ineffectiveness, in turn, can breed frustration, anger, apathy, hopelessness and despair.

Now is the time to empower the would-be social entrepreneur. The current state of international poverty and inequality is well documented: about half the world's population lives on less than two dollars per day, and the majority of the poor live in countries where relative poverty—the gap between the richest and poorest—is increasing. In August 2008, the World Bank overhauled its poverty estimates, incorporating new and better data. Currently, the Bank estimates that at two dollars per day, slightly more than 2 billion people live in poverty worldwide, with 1.4 million of those people

9 Pathways Magazine, (Stanford, CA: Stanford Center on Poverty and Inequality. Fall 2011), 3-7.

living in extreme poverty, defined as $1.25 a day in 2005 prices.[10]

In its February 2010 report, titled Rethinking Poverty, the UN Department of Economic and Social Affairs noted, "The current global financial and economic crisis threatens to wipe out much of the modest progress in poverty reduction since the 2000 Millennium Summit, while climate change increasingly threatens the lives of the poor."[11] Thus, the impact of climate change on the health and welfare of the poorest in developing nations needs immediate addressing.

The UN Development Programme (UNDP), in a report on climate change and the world's most vulnerable, writes, "Developing countries and their poorest citizens are most vulnerable to climate change."[12] Yet the report concludes, "Catastrophic human development setbacks are avoidable."[13] Yes, they are avoidable – with empowered visionary leadership.

In the United States, the picture is likewise alarming. According to the Center on Poverty and Inequality at Stanford University,16 percent of the U.S. population lives in poverty. While a reported 21.9 percent of our children live in poverty, CEOs in our country now make 1,039 times more than the average worker. Residential segregation in our society also is on the rise, and it appears we are

10 Shaohua Chen and Martin Ravallion, *The Developing World Is Poorer than We Thought, but No Less Successful in the Fight Against Poverty, Development Research Group, World Bank,* www-wds.worldbank.org/external/default/WD-SContentServer/IW3P/IB/2010/01/21/000158349_20100121133109/Rendered/PDF/WPS4703.pdf (accessed June 9, 2010).

11 UN Department of Economic and Social Affairs "Rethinking Poverty; Report on the World Social Situation 2010," New York, February 16, 2010, under "Preface," www.un.org/esa/socdev/rwss/docs/2010/fullreport.pdf (accessed June 10, 2010).

12 "Climate Shocks: Risk and Vulnerability in an Unequal World," *UNDP Human Development Report,* (2007/2008), 79.

13 Ibid., 107.

entering a period of prolonged job loss never seen before,[14] with certain ethnic groups being hit harder than others.

The economic realities facing the most vulnerable among us are trending worse. For people mired in poverty and disadvantaged by inequality, one of the few glimmers of hope radiates from people of vision and compassion who dedicate themselves to transformative change.

One such change agent is Marshall Welch, director of the Catholic Institute for Lasallian Social Action, an academic center that promotes a culture of service and social justice education. Here are his thoughts on making change in today's economic landscape, using our methodology:

> The Seven Pillar methodology is a useful framework for thinking about social action. *Vision* provides a sense of direction, a way to gaze out toward the horizon and both wonder and imagine what is waiting out there. Along the way to our future, the Seven Pillars offer us compass points to help guide us. The journey is rarely a straight and simple path; it is fraught with peaks and valleys, twists and turns. Having a broad perspective of that horizon in the distance enables us to notice what lies in our path that may prevent or expedite our journey toward our vision.
>
> Each of us has been given gifts... talents and passions that empower us. We have a responsibility to ourselves and to others to fully utilize those

14   Don Peck, "How a New Jobless Era Will Transform America," *The Atlantic*, March 2010. www.theatlantic.com/magazine/archive/2010/03/how-a-new-job-less-era-will-transform-america/7919/ (accessed April 18, 2010).

special skills. In this sense, we are called to act. This vocation helps us understand and then work to fill the void or chasm that separates and divides us from ourselves and others.

We can use our special skills to build bridges over the chasms. Along the way, we need to take time to reflect on the journey and our efforts. This provides internal feedback loops to help us understand who we are and whose we are.

A true gift is an honest partnership with others, whereby they give external feedback. The insight of others becomes a mirror for us to reflect upon. Likewise, we offer the same candid and caring feedback to our partners. In this way, together we can share the credit of the amazing things we could not accomplish on our own. Our work with others becomes in and of itself a celebration. And through the strong foundation of that partnership, our horizon is expanded, providing a long-term view. Throughout the journey, we can brace ourselves and lean on each other when we encounter bumps along the way.

Welch sees the Seven Pillars as a helpful framework for empowered social action within a conscientious, deliberative community. His perspective is shared by other outstanding social entrepreneurs who are effectively addressing some of today's hardest problems.

OUTSTANDING SOCIAL ENTREPRENEURS

As a benefit of my work at Elfenworks, I have been privileged to meet and work with a number of social entrepreneurs of the highest caliber. These men and women have invested the greater part of their careers in making lasting and measurable change in the lives of thousands upon thousands of people, at home and abroad. Their work has had an impact on fields as diverse as drug addiction rehabilitation, gang intervention, housing the homeless, feeding the hungry, rescuing girls from child prostitution, and putting college within the reach of children who are the first in their families to attain it. Thus their collective expertise includes addiction and recovery, at-risk kids, child prostitution, education, food, safety, hunger and homelessness, peacemaking, solar and sustainability, world health, youth gang intervention, and youth nonviolence.

During the vetting process for Elfenworks' *In Harmony with Hope*^{sm} award, I was gratified to learn how many of the best nonprofits seem to live up to the Seven Pillar criteria, without ever having heard of it. I then looked around at other nonprofits – and even the excellent for-profit organizations with which we were working, and noticed that they, too, met the criteria. Consider these examples:

> **Fr. Gregory Boyle; Homeboy Industries** is
> the largest youth gang intervention program in
> the country, providing addiction and recovery
> programs, a full range of educational services,
> anger management training, etiquette and courtesy
> classes, day care programs (and parenting classes),
> job counseling and placement, and tattoo removal
> services, in addition to all-important skills and job
> training and placement programs. Two hundred
> former gang members help manage and run the

entire operation, which includes a bakery, a café, and silkscreen, maintenance, and retail shops that fund about a third of operations. Fr. Boyle's efforts, which have changed the lives of more than 100,000 people, earned him an Elfenworks Foundation *In Harmony with Hope* award in 2009.

Joyce Dattner; All Stars Project of the SF Bay Area is part of All Stars Project, Inc. a national nonprofit that creates educational and performing arts opportunities outside of school for thousands of poor and minority youth. The group sponsors community and experimental theater, develops leadership training, and pursues volunteer initiatives that build and strengthen communities. The All Stars Project actively promotes supplementary education and the performance-learning model in academic and civic arena. SF Bay Area Director Joyce Dattner was a recipient of an Elfenworks Foundation *In Harmony with Hope* award in 2007.

Robert Egger; DC Central Kitchen was founded with a vision of reworking the food bank model. Instead of providing a simple handout, the Kitchen uses food as a vehicle for change: Clients become employed cooks through the Kitchen's Culinary Jobs Training Program; college students learn about service and business in the Campus Kitchens Project; and 4,500 of DC's hungry are fed as the Kitchen recycles more than one ton of food every day. The Kitchen also provides street outreach and nutrition education for at-risk kids. Founder Robert Egger received an Elfenworks Foundation *In Harmony with Hope* award in 2009.

Rosanne Haggerty; Common Ground and Community Solutions. Common Ground is one of the largest developers of supportive housing in the country. It operates nearly 2,800 apartments in New York City and the surrounding region. Founder Rosanne Haggerty believes fervently that homelessness can be solved. "From city to city, country to country, " she wrote, "the homeless bear a striking similarity. They are the mentally ill; graduates of foster care; those released from prisons and jails without a home or job to go to; victims of domestic violence. We see that the solutions that work in one community can work in others."[15] Haggerty was honored with an *In Harmony with Hope* award in 2010. In her 20 years at Common Ground she created housing and street outreach programs that housed 4,500 individuals and reduced street homelessness in Times Square by 87%. She has since gone from founding Common Ground to found and direct a new nonprofit, Community Solutions, to end and prevent homelessness nationally.

---

15 Rosanne Haggerty, *Ending Homelessness in South Australia*, (South Australian Government - Department of the Premier & Cabinet, Adelaide Thinkers in Residence, Australia, July 2005). http://www.socialinclusion.sa.gov.au/files/Homelessness_Ending.pdf (accessed June 26, 2012).

Dr. Mike Jacobson; Center for Science in the Public Interest has, for more than 40 years, been the preeminent voice for nutrition and health, food safety, alcohol policy, and sound science, boasting the largest circulation health newsletter in North America, the award-winning *Nutrition Action Healthletter*. Co-founder and executive director Michael Jacobson, PhD, and a team of scientist-advocates have worked to educate the public, promote government policies consistent with scientific evidence, and counter industry's powerful influence on public opinion and public policies. Among their accomplishments are Food Day, nutrition labeling and efforts in schools for nutritious lunches and against junk food and soda options. They are working to ensure that all children, no matter their socioeconomic status, have access to healthy and nutritious food daily.

Dr. Lois Lee; Children of the Night is the most comprehensive social service program in North America for American children, ages 11-17, who are victimized by prostitution. Since its inception, the organization has assisted more than 10,000 children who live on the streets and are forced into prostitution to pay for food and a place to sleep. The Program was established as a non-profit in 1979, and is open to child prostitutes throughout the United States, with a hotline ready and able to rescue these children 24 hours a day. Hotline staff work closely with law enforcement officials to rescue children, many of whom are lucky enough to find themselves at the residential home, which features an on-site school and college placement program. Caseworkers are available to provide ongoing case management to hundreds of graduates. Founder Dr. Lee was honored with an *In Harmony with Hope* award in 2008.

Jack McConnell, MD; Volunteers in Medicine explicitly follows the Golden Rule – Do unto others as you would have others do unto you – and the Biblical command to love your neighbor as yourself. Today, they shepherd replication throughout the country, providing access to medical care to patients who otherwise would have none, and an opportunity for service to retirees in the medical community. Since 2001, more than 10,000 medical volunteers have delivered care to nearly one million uninsured people in 90 clinics in 26 states, in a culture of caring, and at no cost to patient or taxpayer. Dr. McConnell's acceptance of an *In Harmony with Hope* award in 2008 was his last public appearance.

Paul Minorini; Boys Hope Girls Hope helps academically capable and motivated but at-risk children in need to meet their full potential through opportunities and education, by working with them until they have graduated from college. Founded in 1977 and based in Bridgeton, Missouri, it now serves 15 cities in the United States, plus Brazil, Guatemala, Mexico and Peru. The nonprofit organization offers everything a healthy family would require – mentoring, education, and financial and moral support – thus, their slogan, "There's no place like hope." President and CEO Minorini was a recipient of an *In Harmony with Hope* award in 2007.

Gary Oppenheimer; AmpleHarvest.org is a nationwide effort that enables America's many millions of home gardeners to easily share their garden bounty with neighbors in need. At its core is a web portal, connecting enrolled food pantries with gardeners nearby. Founder Gary Oppenheimer, a recipient of an *In Harmony with Hope* award in 2012, appreciates the Elfenworks methodology, "I very much appreciate Elfenworks looking towards innovative methodologies, instead of keeping to the way of the past. Your help and that of other people looking at out-of-the-box solutions from outside of their own box will help AmpleHarvest.org and other innovative solutions actually solve some of our nation's problems."

Anna Sidana; One Million Lights is a can-do group, bringing solar lights to the poorest regions of the world. Sidana is using all Seven Pillars at One Million Lights, noting, "The Seven Pillars methodology provides a practical and yet insightful way to approach social entrepreneurship. These pillars offer common-sense thinking to guide you in your strategy, everyday functions and decisions as a leader. They are my safety nets that keep me on the right path." Founding CEO Sidana's vision is reflected in the slogan, "You can change the world if you really want to," as well as in the jingle, "Change you can see, One Million Lights." The organization was incubated at The Elfenworks Foundation before it took wing on its own.

Fr. Peter Young; Peter Young Housing Industries & Treatment (PYHIT) evolved out of Fr. Young's firm belief that effective recovery is only possible if treatment is followed up with housing and job training. With successful public-private partnerships across New York State, programs occupy more than 100 sites. Three thousand people rely on services from PYHIT every day, and it boasts a recidivism rate of less than 10 percent. In all, Fr. Young has helped hundreds of thousands move from addiction to becoming productive members of society. Young was the most entrepreneurial of Elfenworks' 2009 *In Harmony with Hope* award honorees, using funds from the award to underwrite a telethon that garnered $200,000 for his programs. Yet, perhaps due to the stigma associated with prisoners, Young had never before received a foundation grant or award.

When I approached these social entrepreneurial leaders about the Seven Pillars methodology, I was heartened and encouraged by their receptiveness to the methodology. Perhaps the next generation of aspiring change agents will be inspired and guided by such achievement as exemplified by some of the aforementioned founders.

CHAPTER QUESTIONS

1. *Discuss: With which historical entrepreneur did you personally identify? What spoke to you? Can you explain why?*

2. *Name three important characteristics these historical figures had in common. Why did you choose these three, in particular?*

3. *What stood out for you as distinctive differences and similarities among the contemporary social entrepreneurs listed?*

4. *Are there social entrepreneurs you feel were left off this chapter discussion? Who are they, and why should they be included?*

CHAPTER 2 - THE CARTER CONCEPT

INTEGRITY AND INFLUENCE

Jimmy Carter, former governor of Georgia and 39th President of the United States, established the United States Department of Education and worked to develop a national energy policy. He was awarded the Nobel Peace Prize in 2002 for his peace efforts, which included brokering a peace treaty between Israel and Egypt at Camp David. This treaty has been honored to this day, and President Carter has written about it extensively.

Jimmy Carter's presidency was characterized by honesty, integrity, decency and courage. He fostered a spirit of bipartisanship, which didn't arise naturally; he worked for it. And President Carter got more legislation passed than did any other president since President Eisenhower, except President Johnson.

Besides the Panama Canal treaties, SALT II treaty, and Camp David Accords, which are his well-known known accomplishments, President Carter's legacy includes establishing the Department of Energy, protecting national security interests peacefully, appointing more women, African Americans and Hispanics as federal judges than all previous administrations combined; a Mental Health Commission report, passing and funding the Mental Health Systems Act, normalizing diplomatic relations with China, deregulating various industries, controlling toxic wastes through the enactment of Superfund legislation, and brokering the safe return of all American hostages in Iran (they were released on the day President Reagan assumed office).[16]

---

16 "Notable Achievements," Wall Exhibit, The Carter Center Museum and Library, February 2010.

President Carter, it seems, always has been a man of vision, informed by faith. The first openly evangelical president, he continues to make no secret of his life's work as a humble follower of Jesus, based on his understanding of Christianity.

In Andrew Young's spiritual biography of Jimmy Carter, titled *The Carpenter's Apprentice,* Young says President Carter has taught Sunday school since he was 18, teaching every Sunday in the Naval Academy chapel. Young writes of this teaching, "With Jimmy Carter, each lesson leads back to Jesus Christ, to the service of others. 'How would Christ define a successful life for us?' he asks. 'Humility, service, suffering if necessary, and a life full of compassion for unlovable people.'"[17]

President Carter writes, "My basic or traditional beliefs were most persuasively presented to me by my father, who was a deacon and my Sunday school teacher at Plains Baptist Church."[18] His belief as a Baptist emphasizes scriptural passages that "describe how Jesus refrained from giving even his own disciples authority over people. In his charge to them to go out as witnesses, they were empowered only to serve others, by alleviating suffering and espousing truth, forgiveness, and love."[19]

Biographer Daniel Ariail points out that Jimmy Carter has "had the power of a king but still has the heart of a servant."[20] Jimmy Carter and his wife, Rosalynn, embody servant leadership. They attempt to follow the admonition in Micah 6:8 to which Carter alluded in his 1977 presidential inaugural address:

---

17 Andrew Young, *The Carpenter's Apprentice: A Spiritual Biography of Jimmy Carter* (Grand Rapids, MI: Zondervan Books, 1996), 118.

18 Jimmy Carter, *Our Endangered Values* (New York: Simon & Schuster, 2005), 16.

19 Ibid., 17.

20 Dan Ariail and Cheryl Heckler-Feltz, *The Carpenter's Apprentice: The Spiritual Biography of Jimmy Carter* (Grand Rapids, MI: Zondervan Publishing, 1996), 19.

I join in the hope that when my time as your
President has ended, people might say this about
our Nation: that we had remembered the words of
Micah and renewed our search for humility, mercy,
and justice; that we had torn down the barriers
that separated those of different race and region
and religion, and where there had been mistrust,
built unity, with a respect for diversity; that we had
found productive work for those able to perform
it; that we had strengthened the American family,
which is the basis of our society; that we had
ensured respect for the law, and equal treatment
under the law, for the weak and the powerful, for
the rich and the poor; and that we had enabled our
people to be proud of their own Government once
again.

I would hope that the nations of the world might
say that we had built a lasting peace, built not
on weapons of war but on international policies,
which reflect our own most precious values.
These are not just my goals, and they will not be
my accomplishments, but the affirmation of our
Nation's continuing moral strength and our belief
in an undiminished, ever-expanding American
dream.[21]

Underlying President Carter's vision is his understanding of the
true meaning of success. In his GRAMMY® award-winning book,

---

21   Jimmy Carter, Presidential Inaugural Address, Thursday, January 20, 1977,
     www.jimmycarterlibrary.org/documents/speeches/inaugadd.phtml (accessed April
     22, 2010).

Our Endangered Values, President Carter writes of being asked to define success in only 50 words. His response: "I believe that anyone can be successful in life, regardless of natural talent or the environment within which we live. This is not based on measuring success by human competitiveness for wealth, possessions, influence, and fame, but adhering to God's standards of truth, justice, humility, service, compassion, forgiveness, and love."[22]

President Carter is not blindly religious; he has been outspoken regarding the growing crisis of gender violence,[23] the plight of the world's women in general, and the culpability of the world's religions – his own denomination included – in that regard.[24]

President Carter's vision includes a just peace. Most people believe he won a Nobel Peace Prize in 2002 for brokering a peace agreement between Israel and Egypt, but the scope of the prize went beyond the brokering to encompass a lifetime of peacemaking, including the former President's efforts at The Carter Center.

President Carter has written a number of books about the Middle East peace process. He and envoys from The Carter Center regularly visit the region and maintain relations with all the parties with whom an agreement will need to be reached, even if those parties are unsavory and not recognized by the United States government.

THE CARTER CENTER

After leaving the White House, Jimmy and Rosalynn Carter founded The Carter Center, *www.cartercenter.org*, in 1982. They

---

22 Jimmy Carter, *Our Endangered Values*, 28.

23 Stephen Lewis, "A Crisis of Gender Violence," Momentum, www.momentumconference.org/speaker-presentation/speaker/stephen-lewis/presentation/a-crisis-of-gender-violence/index.html (accessed June 10, 2010).

24 Jimmy Carter, "The Words of God Do Not Justify Cruelty to Women," *The London Observer*, July 12, 2009, Web edition: www.guardian.co.uk/commentisfree/2009/jul/12/jimmy-carter-womens-rights-equality (accessed March 5, 2010).

initially considered it an institution for negotiating peace but ultimately expanded its scope. The Center is now a non-partisan, non-governmental organization with a fundamental commitment to human rights and the alleviation of human suffering.

As its tagline, "Waging peace, fighting disease, bringing hope" suggests, Center staff work on conflict resolution and prevention, freedom and democracy, and health and mental-health outcomes. They monitor elections all over the world, fight the stigma of mental illness, and leverage President Carter's elite status as a former president to gain access to public health departments in various countries, with a track record on tackling neglected diseases, second to none.

Their compassionate mission extends beyond visible suffering: the suffering of mental illness. This is Rosalynn Carter's mission. Once she realized she was in a real position to help, she dedicated her life to doing so.

In a letter to me, President Carter described The Carter Center as being guided by the following principles:

> The Center emphasizes action and results. Based on careful research and analysis, it is prepared to take timely action on important and pressing issues. The Center addresses difficult problems and recognizes the possibility of failure as an acceptable risk. The Center is nonpartisan and acts as a neutral party in dispute resolution activities. The Center believes people can improve their lives when provided with the necessary skills, knowledge and access to resources.

The Center has supervised 92 elections in 37 countries. In many of those countries, the Center receives financial support from partner countries, such as the United States, the United Kingdom,

Belgium, Canada, Denmark, Ireland, and Norway.[25] Once a region becomes stable, it is possible for The Center to enter and bring medicines to treat long-neglected disease, such as Mectizan and Albendazole to combat river blindness.

The Center has a vision and is non-duplicative; if others are addressing an issue well, The Carter Center does not enter the space. For example, many other nonprofits are involved with polio eradication, and The Carter Center's specific skills are not needed. Its staff sets their sights only on those neglected areas that fit their special skills, abilities, and partnership possibilities. Sticklers for measurement and for welcoming feedback and course corrections, they gather and use metrics in ways that move their agenda forward. And they have a long-term view that gives them staying power.

I spent a lot of time performing an "appreciative inquiry" of The Carter Center. If I planned to emulate them, I needed to understand how The Center worked. I wasn't disappointed. Visionaries with special skills, fording a chasm with an effective action plan, working in true partnerships over the long-term, measuring for results, and sharing the credit; they uphold the Seven Pillar criteria. I consider them a great role model for other would-be change agents.

The wisdom President Jimmy Carter shared with me – at the time an aspiring social entrepreneur – which I am now sharing with you, invites you to use your vision and special skills in a non-duplicative way, work in partnership with others, give others opportunity to share the credit for results, use a valid feedback loop to measure those results, and allow for bumps in the path as you work over time toward great successes. These are the Seven Pillars.

As with many of the personality tests businesses and educational institutions administer, the Seven Pillars methodology helps you look at your skills and proclivities, and evaluate pursuits

---

25   The Carter Center. "2008-2009 Annual Report." www.cartercenter.org/news/pub-lications/annual_reports.html (accessed March 27, 2011). 30.

for which you would be well suited. Yet the Pillars don't stop there. The methodology explains the challenges individuals will face in their careers. The Pillars combine a variety of management disciplines: picking the best jobs for you, how to succeed in jobs, how to manage within jobs and within your life.

Having and using this framework gives you a greater probability of success, defined as being happy in the job you do, and doing the job well. Life isn't as compartmentalized as we may think; hence the Pillars incorporate the various aspects of business, including career direction, planning, coaching, and management practices.

ILLUSTRATION: MANY DISCIPLINES, SEVEN PILLARS

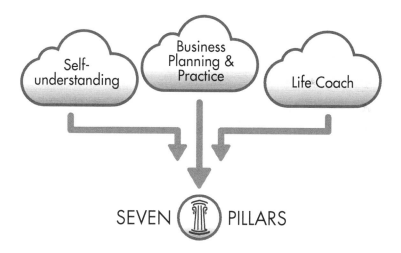

A CARTER CENTER DIFFERENCE

President Carter runs The Carter Center with attention to all Seven Pillars. Yet he has written about another similar set of seven principles, which he also follows. In his book, *Beyond the White House*, he includes 1) non-duplication; 2) non-partisanship; 3) action and direct involvement, not just academic analysis or theory;

4) not allowing fear of failure to be a deterrent from best efforts and worthy chances; 5) not intruding into politically sensitive areas without at least tacit permission from the White House; 6) recognizing the occasional need to name a project generically to allow partners a sense of ownership (e.g., naming the Guinea worm eradication project "Global 2000"); and 7) creating detailed trip reports with copies for leaders in key areas such as the White House.

The first item on The Carter Center list, non-duplication, is the same as our Pillar Three. The fourth, not allowing fear of failure, is suggested in our first Pillar, having a vision that ignores naysayers. The sixth item, generic naming, is a useful tool in valid partnership, our fourth Pillar. The Pillars he discussed with me were tailored to our particular conversation, to the aspiring social entrepreneur.

I considered President Carter's principles as I sought a way to visually represent my Seven Pillars in a way that would be memorable. I tried various options, before settling on the pillar concept. One of them was The Carter Center logo; the eagle with its seven attributes, so I applied one rainbow color to each element of the eagle in a clockwise fashion. But The Carter Center logo didn't feel universally applicable to me, so I let it go, in favor of pillars – an icon which rests upon a solid foundation as it upholds a higher structure – or purpose.

HOW TO RECOGNIZE AND RECALL THE SEVEN PILLARS

Over the years, I have created and discarded various mnemonic devices to help people remember the Seven Pillars . My latest is a short phrase: *Vision and Skill, Unduplicated, Together Share Feedback, Long-term*. It is possible to think of many others; most important is to come up with one that means something to you and connects you to the Seven Pillars.

While I believe there is a chronological order to understanding and implementing the Seven Pillars, I don't find it necessary to keep them in order as you endeavor to remember them. Thus, P.U.R.P.O.S.E. could stand for: Persist (long-term view); Understand (feedback loop); Rave (share credit); Partnership (collaboration); Outlook (vision); Skill-Set (abilities); and Empty Space (chasm or obstacles along the way). Ultimately, what helps most, is a sincere understanding and application of the concepts behind each pillar. Information, once we can explain it, becomes knowledge. Once we can implement it, it becomes skill.

Whether or not you rely on a mnemonic device to remember the Seven Pillars, do understand they involve implementing your *vision* regardless of naysayers, using your *special skills* in a *non-duplicative way*, work in *partnership* with others, giving others opportunity to share the *credit* for results, having a valid *feedback loop* to measure those results, and *allowing for bumps in the path* as you work over time toward great success.

During the next seven chapters, we will examine each Pillar in depth, and consider the methodology as applied by certain visionary social entrepreneurs who have been changing the world with their work.

CHAPTER QUESTIONS

1. *Fill in: The Seven Pillars involve implementing your _____ regardless of naysayers, using your _____ in a _____ way, work in _____ with others, giving others opportunity to share the _____ for results, having a valid _____ to measure those _____, and allowing for _____ as you work over time toward great success.*

2. *Review the Seven Pillars versus the Carter Center Seven Principles. How are they similar?*

3. *Which Pillar seems most important to you right now, and why?*

4. *If you were representing the Pillars in some other way, how might you represent them? A wheel? A star? What would the benefits be, of such a representation, over pillars?*

CHAPTER 3

PILLAR ONE - VISION

Some of our most visionary thinkers are children. Not yet set in their ways or anyone else's, their thinking is less bridled than most adults. Without an established frame of reference, they don't yet assume something won't work, leaving them free to think beyond convention, to fantasize and play "what if?"

Children are masters of make believe, which is an important characteristic of visionary thinking. As Albert Einstein said in 1946, *"a new type of thinking is essential if mankind is to survive and move toward higher levels.*[26]*"*

Visionary change makers see the possibility of a better future and then endeavor to implement that future. The first Pillar is about having that vision. To be an effective social entrepreneur, one who is driving meaningful change, one must first have a vision. One must see it to believe it, must recognize and trust the vision.

The vision involves three components: knowing the problem you want to try to solve, envisioning how you might go about making an impact, and perceiving how things might be different, if you were successful. Having a vision is set out as the first pillar for a reason: as British singer-songwriter Joe Jackson wrote, "You can't get what you want till you know what you want."

Nothing happens without vision and the confidence to trust in that vision. One also must remain oblivious to those corrosive voices, the naysayers who say your goal is impossible to achieve. Tune out the noise and focus on the vision.

---

26 Albert Einstein, quoted in interview with Michael Armrin. "The Real Problem is in the Hearts of Men." *New York Times Magazine.* June 23, 1946.

STEP ONE: LETTING GO

In a world full of competing opportunities for your entrepreneurial attention, it's easy to feel pulled in many directions. A caring heart can feel moved toward many problems, even while the rational mind knows if we were to try to tackle all of them, we could do none of them effectively.

The first step is recognizing a viable vision for change, as we let go of the "impossible" mentality: We cannot, ourselves, fix everything we believe is wrong with the world. We cannot let the mind-numbing and impersonal nature of large numbers stop us: "Don't fail to do something just because you can't do everything."[27] Once we have released ourselves from the need to be superhuman, it becomes possible to really listen to our hearts about what we truly feel is calling to us.

STEP TWO: RECOGNIZING THE VISION

You may be asking yourself, "How do I know, for sure, which area is calling for my involvement?" Look for the telltale signs. Understand it as an area of abiding passion. It touches both your heart and your mind, and it gets you excited. Your speech may become more rapid when you address this topic, and you enjoy engaging in conversations about it. Your friends might describe you as a "deep river" about the topic; an expert whose information flows among them. It captures your imagination, and you actively seek information about it.

Your heart may feel something is not right, and your mind may wander toward possible solutions or questions about why you see none so far. In a world filled with possible focus points, pay

27 Richard Stearns, *The Hole in Our Gospel: What Does God Expect of Us? The Answer That Changed My Life and Might Just Change the World* (Nashville, TN: Thomas Nelson, 2009), 100.

attention to the area in particular that captures your thoughts and your imagination in a palpable way. Sometimes it just makes sense and seems to fit easily within your own skills; it seems designed for you. This happened to Dr. Mike Jacobson of the Center for Science in the Public Interest, who told me:

> Well, we were very young... We wanted to do it
> ourselves and set up an example for other scientists
> on how they could use their scientific knowledge
> outside of the laboratory to advance the public
> interest – to try to get government to do what
> government ought to do and get industry to do
> what it ought to be doing and stop the things it
> shouldn't be doing. And so we did.

STEP THREE: GRADUALLY FALLING IN

Finding your vision may make its logical path over the course of a lifetime. Young change agents starting out, hungry for an "aha!" moment, may find this unsatisfying. Yet rest assured, those who have stayed the course have found their way.

Boys Hope Girls Hope President and CEO Paul Minorini has dedicated more than half his life to the cause, from his time as a "house parent" during college. His vision involves the certainty that children in poverty have as much potential to succeed and learn as do children of privilege, as well as the desire to realize their potential.

STEP FOUR: UNEXPECTED LIFE'S WORK

Although the vision may come gradually into view, it still can come as a surprise, as happened to Dr. Lois Lee, who "fell into" her work at Children of the Night. At the time, Dr. Lee considered herself a radical feminist and was working on her doctoral dissertation, "The Pimp and His Game."

Over time, her activism on behalf of the young women she was researching increased. Then, reportedly, she gave Los Angeles police a lead that resulted in the capture of the infamous Hillside Strangler. During that era, street prostitutes told her about teens working as prostitutes so they could buy cocaine, and madams told her about prominent customers who brought them 16-year-old girls. The madams had daughters the same age, and wanted Dr. Lee to do something to help keep them off the streets.

Up to this point, Dr. Lee's work had focused on adult prostitution and the legal system; although she would step in, in some cases, to try to convince the court to find the young girls guilty, just to give them a place to stay. Yet these girls often ended up back on the streets. Dr. Lee began offering up her own home as shelter.

During the next three years, 250 girls came to stay at her apartment. She heard one of them say, "You wait till she's done with her dissertation; she'll put us back on the street like everyone else." This became her impetus to set up a drop-in shelter and, eventually, a live-in center known as "Children of the Night."

STEP FIVE: THE FORK IN THE ROAD

Some of us, rather than gradually falling into an area that fits us, come suddenly upon a fork in the road, which presents us with choices, and invites us to make a decision. Former nightclub manager Robert Egger, founder of DC Central Kitchen, believes we reach this crossroads most often without the assistance of a signpost saying, "Love and happiness this way." Nevertheless, the road less taken is both evident and essential. He should know; it happened to him, and he took a chance.

Egger's moment came when he realized that giving out sandwiches for his church didn't do enough; a cold sandwich didn't bring these people in from the cold. He chose to go against his assumed destiny of opening another nightclub, and instead established DC Central Kitchen, an organization that "uses food as a tool to strengthen our community through job training, meal distribution and supporting local food systems."

"I've always felt," he said, "that once your eyes were opened to something, you had an obligation; you couldn't just look away. I saw how we have to make things right, and that involved getting people back on their feet, and working for justice." [28]

STEP SIX: TRUSTING THE VISION

Once you have your vision in sight, how do you know you can trust it? This is an inspired vision, but is it the one you want to invest in? Former President Ronald Reagan made famous the phrase, "Trust but verify." In that spirit, consider ways in which you might get input on your thought process.

Friends are a terrific resource in helping us to know ourselves better and discern our vision. Ask what topic they see you really passionate about. Do you follow the popular causes, or do they recognize in you a persistent concern for another specific area?

Your own time use is another indicator. We naturally tend to spend time on pursuits of passion. Ask yourself, "Do my social media posts have a common thread, and does this thread lead me to my vision? Where do I find myself speaking up or joining in? What path do I already seem to be following?

Finally, techniques used in many faith traditions can be useful in discerning an authentic call to action. Consulting someone in

---

28   Robert Egger. Interview by Lauren Speeth, March 8 with follow-up September 29, 2010.

your tradition may provide additional insight.

Once you are certain you are passionate about a vision and can articulate it, stop questioning, and start looking for ways to realize it. We need to be our own allies, not become naysayers to our own vision.

STEP SEVEN: TRUSTING THE VISIONARY SELF

One reason many people do not trust their vision is they somehow don't trust that they, themselves, could be the person to lead the charge for change. I call this false humility, as distinguished from the true humility that realizes and accepts it takes a village to actually make change. This puts me in mind of advice I once received from Br. Ed Phelan, the Christian Brother who is spiritual leader of the Lasallian Volunteers, a USA-Toronto-based organization dedicated to empowering the poor by training volunteers to provide personalized education services.

Br. Phelan, quoting English writer G.K. Chesterton, said, "If something is worth doing, it is worth doing badly." He meant that it's up to us to do the best we can, rather than waiting for some super human to do a perfect job. If you have seen something and consider it worth doing, go ahead and implement it. Don't wait for perfection; there is no one better to implement your inspired vision than you.

Just because you are not an accomplished musician doesn't mean you must abandon your vision of joining the orchestra. Cello lessons await. Don't let false constructs stand in your way of realizing your dream.

Chesterton also said, "To have a right to do a thing is not at all the same as to be right in doing it." Know yourself, choose your visions wisely, and then trust them.

STEP EIGHT: SHARING DOUBTS... WISELY

Once you have set upon your work, you still may have doubts about your vision. The choice of a few wise counselors in whom you can confide is critical to success. They can keep you on a positive path, and help you steer your course. However, confiding your doubts in the team you have assembled can be ruinous: you can create your own naysayers. As Rosanne Haggerty of Community Solutions puts it:

> Everyone's looking for innovation as well, but you're not rewarded for sharing your doubts. To admit from the get-go would be very healthy, but there are reasons people are wary of that because it's not rewarded. You're trying to help someone see a vision of something that doesn't exist yet, and you're showing how achievable that vision is, so talking about the risks and likely detours and delays is discordant with the vision that you're putting out there.

> These days, especially after the financial crisis, everyone's looking for a sure thing... There's a fascination with the new, exciting and successful, without appreciation for the very real discomfort that needs to be taken on if you're going to move forward. Any successful change agent has worked through this, but it is lonely.

STEP NINE: KNOWING THE NAYSAYERS

Before you tune them out entirely, it may be worthwhile to take a quick look at the naysayers, to understand what motivates them. It simply may be fear, either for you or for them. If you can understand them, perhaps you can sway them, but at least achieving an understanding can help you clarify your position and work to strengthen your own resolve.

Anna Sidana, founder of One Million Lights, added this insight, "This one is tricky because it is often the people we respect and trust who end up being the naysayers. But I think they are driven more by fear, while you have to keep yourself motivated and focused on the opportunity and the cause. Also, it takes a certain kind of individual to take a risk and make a leap of faith. Most naysayers are risk averse and unable to see the big picture."

STEP TEN: VISION, AGENDAS EVOLVE

Go into your work with an understanding that your agenda will evolve. Consider The Carter Center, which was first envisioned as a location where they would forge peace agreements, such as the 1978 peace treaty negotiations between Egypt and Israel President Carter brokered at Camp David. Heads of State came to realize they might be able to make a greater contribution, including international peace efforts, mental health, and fighting neglected disease.

At Elfenworks, I started with a vision of "elves behind the scenes" assisting other efforts, but grew to realize we could be initiators of change, at the forefront, with our own programs. So too, your vision should be flexible and resilient, as you grow with confidence to create change in the world.

STEP ELEVEN: TUNING OUT NAYSAYERS

To succeed, one must have unwavering vision and be oblivious to those corrosive voices that say your goal is impossible to achieve. Previous successes can help; they will protect you against naysayers in your new social entrepreneurial endeavor.

Take a good look at your history, seeking out previous successes. Write them down to strengthen your resolve against the naysayers who inevitably will arise. You may want to take out an old résumé, and consider your successes in the working world, but other successes can be equally useful. Dr. Donald Hopkins, author of *The Greatest Killer, Smallpox in History*,[29] was strategic in the eradication of that disease and is now overseeing the health programs, including the Guinea Worm eradication effort, at The Carter Center.

Once, following a presentation I made on the Seven Pillar methodology at The Carter Center, Dr. Hopkins spoke. During his lecture, he referred to my presentation and to his experience with naysayers, specifically noting that he had been inoculated against naysayers with his experiences eradicating smallpox. Now, as Guinea worm is being eradicated, he feels participants also are being immunized to naysayers. But you don't have to eradicate smallpox to be inoculated against naysayers. If your example of disproving naysayers is having created a fat-free tiramisu when everyone thought this was impossible, by all means, use it to fortify your message.

On another occasion, at a lunch I attended with Dr. Hopkins, he addressed a teen at our table. "Never, he said, "let anyone from my generation tell you what you're trying to do is impossible. I used to get that all the time, but now people don't say that to me so much, anymore."

Indeed, they would not. Dr. Hopkins, like President Carter, is a transformational leader, which I define as "dreamers in action with no ears for naysayers." Dr. Hopkins doesn't see an issue apart from the best and most beautiful possibilities for resolution. He also envisions a path to get there and is building it, one stepping

---

29   Hopkins, Donald. *The Greatest Killer, Smallpox in History*. Chicago, IL Chicago University Press, 2002.

stone at a time. Somehow, he and his team balance a "resistance is futile" mindset with an openness to other points of view, allowing for feedback and forward movement.

Transformational leaders work to create authentic and just peace, taking a broad view of the stakeholders and their deep needs. In all cases, the fundamental vision is there.

STEP TWELVE: ACT ON YOUR VISION

A vision, without a plan of action, is merely a dream.

I rest my case.

CHAPTER QUESTIONS

1. *Discuss: The author writes that the first step in recognizing the vision is letting go of the need to be superhuman. Is this true, in your own experience? Give an example of your own mortal message.*

2. *Identify three areas in which you might envision yourself an agent of change, by asking friends or reviewing your social media posts.*
   A. *What do you see as your vision areas?*
   B. *Is there one that stands out in particular?*
   C. *How did this vision arrive in your life?*
      As an "Aha?"
   D. *Gradually? Discuss.*

3. *Inoculate yourself against naysayers. Discuss previous successes in life and times when you had received but dismissed negative input.*

CHAPTER 4

PILLAR TWO - SPECIAL SKILLS

As a member of an orchestra, I've watched a lot of soloists from behind the scenes. I'm often stunned by the soloists, particularly their strength, stamina and beauty and power of their musical "voices" to evoke emotion in the audience. This seems especially true of opera singers. I have read about the precision and mastery of the cardiac surgeon to restart a beating heart. I have seen the passion and power of the athlete going for gold. I have witnessed a judge apply an alchemy of critical thinking and compassion to restore justice.

I am not nor will I ever be an opera singer, cardiac surgeon, Olympic athlete, judge. Fortunately, no one expects this of me. I have infinite admiration of the skills behind each, and I have an acute understanding of my own special skills.

I have an ability to research, to analyze, to code, to debug, to write, to motivate, to inspire, to envision change, and to network and gather the collaborative talent to make it happen. I never lament what I can't do; I simply call upon those who can.

Every one of us has special skills and brings a unique set of problem-solving abilities to his or her vision. These skills go beyond our job titles and often extend further than our sense of self. Consider the way we think, behave and interact; imagine the various categories of ability:

- Knowledge and Technical Skill: The way we operate: verbal, cultural, musical and electronic literacy, as well as numeracy and language fluency.
- Cognition: The way we think; judging, perceiving, active learning, wonder, critical and logical thinking, analytical and spatial thinking, problem solving, decision making,

mathematics, musicality, systems analysis and evaluation, planning, troubleshooting and envisioning.

- Character: The way we are; honesty, integrity, loyalty, resiliency, flexibility, adaptability, punctuality, attention to detail, reliability, dependability, responsibility, professionalism, confidence, enthusiasm, independence, conscientiousness, work ethic, outlook, hope and grounding in faith tradition.

- Interpersonal Skill: The way we interact; bridge building, coaching, counseling, delegating, peacemaking, negotiating, advocacy, asserting, managing conflict, managing groups, persuading, instructing, active listening, service orientation, leadership, rapport development, social perceptiveness, promoting change and public speaking.

- Social and Financial Capital: The way we leverage resources; the ability to bring financial resources to bear on an issue of concern, convening power.

THE AREA OF COMPETITIVE ADVANTAGE

In the business world, any area where your organization exceeds others is known as your "competitive advantage." This is what the Special Skills Pillar addresses. Although it is possible to improve your skills or acquire new ones, it is not the same or as efficient as developing the team that will compensate for your weaknesses, so you can play to your strengths. Your true competitive advantage lies in being realistic about your strengths and your weaknesses, and filling in with those who complement you.

RECOGNIZING THE SKILL SET

When seeking to bring about change, it is important to assess your skill set honestly, and evaluate those of your organization.

Taking time to reflect on your skills, vocational interests and inspired causes is worth the investment.

One of the most useful tools for gaining insight into my own personal landscape was the "Strong Vocational Interest Inventory," administered by a college counseling center years ago. I am still amazed by how well it predicted the arenas and jobs I was primed to pursue, and where I would thrive and make a difference. The Internet also introduces many tools, as well as additional information on self-assessment quizzes. You can search for "Meyers Briggs," for example, or find several sites offering tests for free. When you search online, beware of rogue websites. Surf safely.

A FEW EXAMPLES

Some of us encounter our life's work early. For example, Brenda Eheart, Ph.D., founder of Generations of Hope, was always drawn to child welfare, and especially the welfare of child wards of the court. In the 1990s, when serving as Director of the Developmental Child Care Program at the University of Illinois in Champaign, she focused her research on the foster care system, and what might make subsequent adoptions more successful. Her moment of epiphany came as she witnessed a judge grant a family's request to undo an adoption, and considered the child's perspective. Looking into the court records, she learned that the child shared a birthday with her own daughter. The thought that this child would learn the news while being picked up after school spurred her resolve to develop a completely different way of caring for our vulnerable kids.

For others of us, it can take a while to figure out what our special skills are and are not, what we want to do and not do. We must become sufficiently self-aware to have assessed our special skills. I recall the time when I was a stay-at-home mom and, meaning well, baked brownies for a local fundraiser. Ask my family, and they will laugh and tell you I have more skills with a computer than with a kitchen. Legend has it I can burn water. I once caused a Pyrex dish to explode. I don't think I was very self-aware when I volunteered for that assignment. But my heart was in the right place. I admit, I wanted immediate, tangible results. It was good to feel as if people were actually being fed by my own hands.

Still, it was not the most effective use of my skills and training and, ultimately, not what would have made me feel the most fulfilled. I had a doctorate in business administration. That organization would have been so much better off had I lent them even an hour of my expertise than they were in receiving the few dollars we raised through the sale of my home-baked brownies. Of course, the whole problem may have been the brownies.

Consider instead how the luthier John F. Mello went about the same problem: he produced a CD of his guitarist clients playing guitars he made, to bring with him to guitar shows. He gives out copies in return for a check written directly to whatever food pantry is nearby the show. He also has has left the CD with restaurants, again with proceeds to benefit the hungry. When I mentioned the possibility of including his example in the book, he was reluctant. He pointed out that he, too, benefited from people hearing his guitars, well played, and added "it's not all that wonderful; steady but quite modest in comparison with what others do." But the fact is, he's doing *something...* and his solution fits his skill-set perfectly[30].

What am I saying? Knowledge is purposeful; knowledge applied is power. And if you can't bake brownies, it is better to buy them than burn them – or sell something else, or give the assignment to someone who can. Play to your strengths. Give in ways where you can make your greatest contribution.

---

30 John Mello. Interview by Lauren Speeth, June 25, 2012.

Later, volunteering to help a group of Russian immigrants proved a better match for me, even though I don't speak Russian. I knew a few languages – Portuguese, Spanish, German, French, and a little Italian – but not Russian. Even though there was no need for the languages I knew in that particular volunteer opportunity, I did have other skills. I had a certificate from college in teaching English as a second language that helped me when working with non-native speakers. In all, it wasn't such a bad match of skills and assignment. Certainly, it was better than the brownies. But again, it wasn't ideal.

Only when I understood and embraced my vision, and aligned it with my skills set did I realize that to be an effective social entrepreneur involved leveraging my efforts in a larger, solutions-oriented way. I recognized in myself skills that would help – computer programming, multimedia and bridge-building skills, combined with an entrepreneurial spirit and strong work ethic.

I thought a team of like-minded individuals might be effective in social entrepreneurship and, in 2005, we went on to create The Elfenworks Foundation. I realized my Silicon Valley technical skills would be useful in an area I cared about: fostering hope in America. Additionally, by continuing to pursue education and training, I have further honed my skills set to be more effective in implementing my vision.

Don't discount any skill until you are certain it doesn't apply. Language skills, for example, are extremely important for international work, and can be helpful domestically as well. At Elfenworks, we have put our language skills to work on many projects, including The Butterfly Project, a multi-lingual set of online resources to help kids under stress reduce stress cortisol, a hormone that is toxic to growing brains.

One Million Lights creator Anna Sidana has found fluency in Hindi useful when she travels to remote regions in India. And she has brought many other skills to her work; for example, her skills as a parent helps her forge relationships with schools. And she applies a strong background in negotiation to her work. No skill should be overlooked or discounted when developing or presenting your vision.

SPECIAL SKILLS AS THE CORNERSTONE

Sometimes, special skills are the entire base upon which an organization is created. Partners In Health is one example. Another is Volunteers in Medicine. Created by a retired doctor, it puts the special skills of its volunteers – retirees from the medical community – at the service of the needy. Likewise, former nightclub manager Robert Egger relied on his food services industry expertise when creating DC Central Kitchen.

The same is true of Elfenworks, a team of technologists, musicians, filmmakers, storytellers, and bridge builders with a varied skill set that includes many aspects of technology and media. In addition, I see our mindset as a special feature; I describe it as a "Silicon Valley" mentality. It is entrepreneurial and somewhat risk-taking, embraces technology, dares to dream big dreams and ventures into the unknown.

When I envision where a project can lead, and see how my skills will help bring it about, I become very excited. I have hopes of someday creating a "Museum of Living Hope," for example, to inspire potential social entrepreneurs. And a few years back, I became really enthusiastic about a socially responsible business project called Fair Truth. This grass-roots initiative, I believed, could help create local abundance by assisting providers of American-made goods and services in alerting consumers about their "fair truth" practices regarding employees and the environment, and enabling interested consumers to vote with their pocketbooks.

I began spearheading this effort in 2006. Rather than build it first and see who might use it, we decided to work in a stepwise way. We convened a conference on possibilities, and are now working to understand consumer interest.

I still find myself constantly reignited by the possibilities for business as a force for good, particularly as this area continues to pull on many of my skills, including my business acumen, computer programming and bridge building. This is what happens when skills and vision align.

THE WAY WE THINK – MINDSET AS SKILL SET

Generally, when thinking of our skills, we consider our training and innate abilities. But why not include our mind – the way we think – as well? Are we naturally good at problem solving or logical or spatial thinking? Are we analyzers or doers? Is planning a skill or a blank area? What sort of learner are we?

Consider Albert Einstein, whose open mind and ability to wonder set the foundation for his discoveries. Whether we consider the expansive mind an attribute or an actual way of thinking, it would be useful to examine the way we think and what it may reveal.

Perhaps you possess the ability to be flexible, to maintain an open mind. I consider that a skill. Our mindset is such an important attribute that I never close an interview with a candidate for funding without asking questions to establish whether he or she is able to think about creative solutions and to wonder about possibilities.

Gil Crawford, CEO of MicroVest, a microfinance investment firm providing capital to financial institutions that serve low-income populations, believes that an essential asset to run an effective nonprofit is a mindset that enables risk-taking when there is a potential for high rewards. In the world of foundations, he calls this "venture philanthropy," and he finds it both essential and rare. MicroVest is a for-profit entity that is owned by a group of these rare nonprofits (CARE USA, MEDA, Cordes Foundation and Seed Capital Development Fund) that realized that investment in low-income financial institutions are best made from a for-profit platform, and that their philanthropic capital can have catalytic impact by seeding groups such as MicroVest. Since risk-taking is not typically built into the system, it is up to us to create such a culture, particularly at a time it is most desperately needed. Otherwise, Crawford sees a medieval court, where non-profits act like courtiers, advancing closer to the king by putting others down to access the limited supply of philanthropic capital.

To Crawford, the venture capitalist is to the commercial banker what the venture philanthropist is to the foundation staff. Crawford notes that foundations are like many commercial bankers, reluctant to take risk:

> "They operate... unwilling to take risk. The people they are funding with philanthropic dollars are [at the helm of] nonprofits. Because they both operate in a world of limited resources, they tend to come to the same conclusions... In the for-profit world, we expect a few failures. Not so, in the nonprofit world. There is no upside for a foundation or government to take risk. We need to create venture philanthropists who are rewarded or penalized based on measurable objectives."

Perhaps a mindset which embraces optimism and hope, and which can be unashamedly idealistic, also is an asset, fostering the perception of possibilities where others see problems. It is this mindset that has enabled Elfenworks to reach out to establish first-of-their-kind partnerships and programs with Mills College, Saint Mary's College,

Stanford, Harvard and Golden Gate universities, Campus MovieFest, and others, and to develop in-house programs as well.

It is this same mindset that enables The Carter Center to go after dreaded diseases, such as Guinea worm, for as long as it takes, to eradicate them.

LACKING THE SKILLS

What if you don't feel you have the requisite skills to work in an area in the way you envision? You can go get the skills. You can train. You can learn by doing. You can bring in those who do. Or you can reassess what skills you have, and use them now, in a way that works toward your vision. Many of the change agents whose stories you admire didn't start out knowing how to do what they do now.

When Fr. Greg Boyle first became a young Jesuit, he probably wasn't ready to become the founder of Homeboy Industries. He became ready slowly, over time, through teaching teens at Loyola High School in Los Angeles, fulfilling pastoral duties at Dolores Mission in Boyle Heights, and working as a chaplain at Islas Marias Penal Colony in Mexico and at Folsom Prison in California. You don't have to jump in the deep end; you can follow Fr. Boyle's example and swim slowly and steadily, with deliberate strokes toward your goal.

LATENT SPECIAL SKILLS

Sometimes, the skills necessary for success become apparent only after you have become involved with a cause. This was true for Dr. Michael Jacobson, cofounder of the Center for Science in the Public Interest, a Washington, D.C.-based nonprofit advocacy for nutrition and health, food safety, alcohol policy and sound science.

Skilled as a scientist, Dr. Jacobson did not know he had skills as an advocate or author. Today, his award-winning newsletter, *Nutrition Action*, has 900,000 subscribers. Nowadays, he applies not only his special skills as a scientist but also the latent skills he developed to become an author and advocate:

> I didn't know what skills I had. I have a PhD in molecular biology, so I spent basically four years in the laboratory, not doing social advocacy. I was fortunate I had these hidden skills. As I got into food issues, starting with consumer advocate Ralph Nader, I started writing a book. I never knew I could write a book , particularly one on understanding corporate motives and learning about bureaucracies and how to collaborate with other organizations.

> I learned, along with the other two fellows with whom I established CSPI, how to start an organization and turn it into an effective advocacy organization. Two years before, I was washing test tubes. These latent skills I never before had an occasion to use, were there. If they weren't, I still would be washing test tubes.

Similarly, Dr. Jack McConnell, founder of Volunteers in Medicine, had the medical skills but quickly realized, when tackling the legal and political challenges associated with operating free clinics and working with volunteers, that he also had another important skill: the gift of persuasion.

SPECIAL SKILLS OBVIOUS TO EVERYONE BUT YOU

Sometimes, your special skills are so obvious to everyone else that others must point them out before you perceive them yourself. This happened to Rev. Peter Young, founder of Peter Young Housing Industries and Treatment, which offers alcohol and substance abuse treatment and transitional housing programs.

Young recalls, when he was in the Navy and on shore leave one evening, other men were getting drunk, taking advantage of the women. He wouldn't stand for it. He was pretty big back then, and he got into fights over it. On deck the next day, his commanding officer said,

> "Yeoman, you are bleeding."
> "Sir, yes Sir," he responded.
> "Why are you bleeding?"
> "The men were disrespecting the women, Sir; I couldn't have that, Sir."
> "You should be a chaplain. Think about it."
> "Sir, yes Sir."

Young thought that was the end of it, but his commanding officer didn't let it go. Soon after that incident, Yeoman Young was given his orders and was told there was no use arguing: it had all been arranged. The Navy had perceived his special skills, and had ordered him into his life of service.

Rev. Young went on to become a program founder in the addiction recovery movement in New York, which preaches and practices treatment over incarceration. He attended countless civic meetings because he was set like a bulldog to decriminalize alcohol addiction. This was at a time when it was punishable by imprisonment to be caught inebriated in public in New York. Because of Rev. Young, that law went national.

In 2009, we sent a member of our team to film Rev. Young for that year's *In Harmony with Hope* award. We captured the story of a man I'll call Dan, a brilliant, articulate young man whose parents were "deadheads." He told how he had begun shooting up at age 5 to gain some control over his life, to keep others from shooting him up. Free from addiction in his late 20s, Dan is looking forward to living on his own and has found his brother, too. His is just one of many stories of lives changed by Rev. Young in his more than 50 years of rescuing people.

Now in his 80s, Rev. Young is as active as ever, even as his work often presents him with real danger. He once emailed me after he had rescued someone whose tongue some drug pushers had tried to pull out. Young offers the protection of 100-plus residential homes scattered around New York State, enabling many addicts to feel safe in coming under his wing.

A KEY TO HAPPINESS

For success, the Seven Pillar methodology advises working within one's skill set. This doesn't mean to rest on one's laurels. We all can benefit from broadening our skills. This is important, not only to entrepreneurial success; this is an important life lesson for happiness, too.

How many of us yearn for a life for which we are not well suited? I know I did, for many years. I now recognize that the obsessive tendencies that served me so well as a computer programmer make me ill-suited to my childhood dream.

As a child, I wanted tremendously to be a traveling doctor, flying in a helicopter to where troubled people were suffering. I would study my Physician's Desk Reference and dream of days spent in a white coat, helping others. But in high school, when I couldn't bear to cut up a frog, my hopes were dashed. I now know I do well in an office and would feel less fulfilled in a disorganized, rural environment. But I didn't always know this about myself.

Perhaps a wise high school counselor, if I had only met one, could have steered me toward a career in epidemiology, the study of the characteristics and distribution of health-related events. The same vision – healing the world – can be realized in many ways, some of which are better suited than others to one's nature.

CHAPTER QUESTIONS

1. *Review the list "The Way We Think." What are the attributes of the way you think? Are you a logical thinker, or more of a free-flowing thinker? Do you enjoy planning, evaluating, or troubleshooting?*

2. *Review the list "The Way We Are." Discuss your impressions with a colleague.*

3. *Locate your top three areas of special skills, through critical thinking, asking friends, and reviewing any skills quizzes available:*

4. *What do you see as your skills areas and in what areas do you not see yourself?*

5. *In what type of environment are you most comfortable or uncomfortable?*

6. *Consider: What latent skills would you like to discover, in yourself? How can you find out if you have any abilities in this area?*

7. *What would you list for "knowledge and skill"? Have you any plans for adding to this list? If so, what is the timeframe for adding to this list? Make a real plan.*

8. *What baby step can you take, this week, to either learn more about your skills and proclivities, or improve them? Commit to taking that step.*

CHAPTER 5

PILLAR THREE - NON-DUPLICATION

Starbucks seems to know what they're doing. A handful of other coffee chains also seem to be brewing good business, but they don't have nearly the market share owned by Starbucks. Ten to twenty years ago, while the Three Tenors enjoyed world renown, was not the ideal time for other, up-and-coming tenors to achieve success. Unless they sang pop.

What am I getting at? If the aspiring entrepreneur does not have a new idea, he or she had better come up with a variation on a theme. We already have sliced bread. And bagels.

The third Pillar, non-duplication, refers to the principle that if someone is doing something *well*, there is no need to duplicate the work. This is similar, in the business world, to finding a market niche. It makes no sense for a new business to enter a saturated market – unless you truly can improve upon what is there. You can't invent the mouse trap, but perhaps you can build a better one. Find a niche where you are needed. The same holds true in for-profit and nonprofit business under the tenets of this Pillar.

CORPORATIONS AND NICHE STRATEGIES

In the business world, corporations seek profit using various strategies to capture a share of the market in their area of operation. If managers aren't doing something really innovative, they still need to somehow go beyond others, to differentiate themselves, perhaps by being wildly faster, better, or cheaper than the competition. By asking "how much faster, better, or cheaper can I do this?" a manager can discern whether a need is already being met effectively, or whether jumping in could be profitable and add value. If so, a strategic plan is warranted.

But beware of simplistic rules about doing more with less; the incentive to cut costs or speed results can cause unintended consequences. Dr. Scott Hubbard, the former director of the NASA Ames Research Center, cautions that "lean management, tight budgets and minimal checks and balances (are) not always wise,"[31] and that "faster, better, cheaper" should be applied only "where it makes sense and where it is prudent."[32] Efficiency should never be confused with effectiveness.

After the mission (vision) and internal assessment of strengths and weaknesses (skills) are known, a marketplace analysis should be undertaken. To interpret the external landscape, a business needs to understand thoroughly, not just its goals and its customers, but also who its competitors are, what threats might exist, and whether there are any barriers to competition not yet in play.

All strategic analysis used in the business world is relevant to the social entrepreneur. Different language will be used; where the business world sees customers, the social entrepreneur may identify clients, patients, colleagues or fellow citizens, but in both cases, the end user will influence and, ideally, benefit from your product or service. Where the business person sees competitors, the social entrepreneur may, in the best cases, see potential partners.

Just as the business executive does, the nonprofit executive may see a landscape filled with potential, clear-cut solutions and yet choose not to proceed. Or, she may sense success and want a part of it. Dr. Lois Lee, founder of Children of the Night, the country's oldest and most reputable non-prison program rescuing children from the nightmare of child prostitution, has pointed out[33] that when

---

31 Scott Hubbard, *Exploring Mars*. Tuscon, AZ: University of Arizona Press, 2011, 42.

32 Ibid., 59.

33 Lois Lee. Interview by Lauren Speeth, March 17, 2010.

people want to duplicate good work, it is not always for altruistic intentions. Sometimes, wherever the funding is, that's where the program will spring up.

Profit-seekers may see you on television, may realize there is government money involved, and may begin chasing after funding they believe is available, without understanding the intention, the skill, the work required, or without having the best interests of the vulnerable population at heart. Yet sometimes, people simply trust and believe they can do it better. And so they should.

NONPROFITS AND NON-DUPLICATION

The best nonprofits fill a chasm. Homeboy Industries of Los Angeles, for example, is the country's largest gang intervention program. Father Greg Boyle, founder of Homeboy, agrees strongly with the importance of seeking to fill a chasm:[34]

> Certainly, we all needed to "fill a chasm" when "felony-friendly employers" were not forthcoming. Homeboy Bakery was born because the situation was too urgent to wait for employers to hire gang members. We had to do it ourselves.

> Now, that chasm has become a secure base – the place where attachment happens among folks for whom attachment is foreign. Without a secure base and the experience of attachment, it is hard for gang members to find the resilience that will enable them to re-identify and re-direct their lives.

The Carter Center is another distinctive, non-duplicative nonprofit. Their unique skills include peacemaking and global

---

34   Gregory Boyle, SJ. Interview by Lauren Speeth, March 8, 2010.

72

public health, but they only will establish a program if someone else isn't already in the space and doing a good job. Among a host of things they do not do is environmental work, clean water, AIDS, polio and disaster relief because so many other organizations are addressing those efforts effectively. They do partner occasionally in the field with organizations that bore wells to provide clean water sources for the villages they work in, but they do not fund them.

Another Georgia nonprofit, Access to Capital for Entrepreneurs, provides microloans and expertise to build small businesses, including America's poorest rural areas. I asked founder Grace Fricks whether, when she started out, anyone else was creating access to capital in her area, and she answered,

> No, there was not. In fact, not only was no one
> doing microfinance in Appalachia but, in Georgia,
> we're still the only ones there. Today there are
> fewer CDFIs (Community Development Financial
> Institutions) in the southeastern U.S. than in any
> other region in the country. Several are joining
> together to collaborate in hopes that we can
> educate people about who we are and what we do
> to move people and places out of poverty.[35]

Another example of non-duplication can be found at The Center for Science in the Public Interest. Founder Dr. Jacobson notes that the center has intentionally stayed away from certain areas.

> We have always tried to work on issues that are
> significant and that others aren't working on; for
> instance, tobacco. That's just a scourge; cigarette
> smoking. So many groups are doing it, and we

---

35   Grace Fricks. Interview by Lauren Speeth, May 21, 2010.

have never figured out a way to get involved and contribute something unique.

Non-duplication involves assessing the space and knowing who the players are. An assessment study by the management consulting firm McKinsey & Company concluded, this "gives The Carter Center a distinctive, skill-based advantage relative to peer organizations. Other organizations rate high along one or two of the core skills, but only The Carter Center combines high levels of all three: academic knowledge, application-oriented programs, and access to world leaders."[36]

Oprah Winfrey established a leadership academy for girls in South Africa. Other leadership academies exist in the world and are doing good work. But Oprah filled a chasm in a time and place for a population that had no access to such opportunity. Her idea was not new. But the where and why and for whom she implemented it was ground breaking.

What is it about your idea that truly will make a difference? After all, is it visionary if it's already being done?

---

36 McKinsey & Company, Inc., "Developing an Effective Management Organization: The Carter Center," Fellows and Senior Staff Retreat, December 11, 1992, 8.

CHAPTER QUESTIONS

1. *What makes an idea visionary?*

2. *Choose a business space (e.g., running shoes, grocery stores). On a blank piece of paper, write down four companies that are in this space. Do they compete? How do they overlap? What makes each unique?*

3. *Consider a company that tried to take over a space that had others in it. Did it work?*

4. *What do you see as a down-side of a "faster, better, cheaper" mindset? How can the incentive to do more with less bring about trouble?*

5. *Choose a social entrepreneur space (e.g., clean water, public health, sustainability, peace). Write down four nonprofits that are in this space. Do they compete? How do they overlap? Where are they unique?*

CHAPTER 6

PILLAR FOUR - PARTNERSHIP

Consider Gilbert & Sullivan, Wozniak & Jobs, Franklin & Eleanor, Barnum & Bailey, Baskin & Robbins, Watson & Holmes. Working in valid partnership with other stakeholders is a key to success, and the fourth of the Seven Pillars.

Michael D. Eisner and Aaron R. Cohen, in their book, *Why Great Partnerships Succeed*, say, "Dig deep, and you will find the most compelling argument for working together: happiness."[37] Although the definition of happiness might be broadened to include shared vision, sense of purpose and balance of responsibility, is there more to it than that?

According to Mark Benioff and Carlye Adler, authors of *The Business of Changing the World: Twenty Great Leaders on Strategic Corporate Philanthropy*, corporate philanthropic foundations are a powerhouse for change, expending more than $30 billion, annually. But, the authors suggest, to be truly successful, these foundations leverage all their assets for maximum effectiveness.[38] Nonprofit organizations also must consider how to leverage their clients, products and partners.

HAVING THE EYES FOR PARTNERSHIP

What if you could see partnership potential everywhere? Some of the most creative change makers do just that. For example, Dr. Lois Lee, founder of Children of the Night, is constantly on the

---

37 Michael D. Eisner and Aaron R. Cohen, *Why Great Partnerships Succeed* (New York, NY: Harper Collins 2010)

38 Marc Benioff and Carlye Adler, *The Business of Changing the World: Twenty Great Leaders on Strategic Corporate Philanthropy* (New York, NY: McGraw-Hill, 2007), xxii.

lookout for potential partners.

> I have very unique partnerships that most people
> don't have. I have high-end hair stylists in Beverly
> Hills salons, for example, so when these kids get
> their hair done, they're sitting next to stars. I have
> the optometrist to the stars; I have 150 people like
> that. And I'm not letting any stone go unturned...
> My optometrist asked me, 'What do you need?' so I
> asked for help. People can tell if your heart is in it.

Dr. Lee also works with more commonplace partners, including the children themselves, plus police, FBI, victim advocates, free clinics (e.g., Planned Parenthood), and universities, for therapy and counseling. Her vision for creative partnership has paid big dividends.

Long before working in public-private partnerships became a well-accepted practice, Sustainable Conservation, a California nonprofit working to protect the environment, was a pioneer in partnering with business, including agriculture. Executive Director Ashley Boren, explains what prompted her organization to take this path, and why it has been successful:

> We believe a lot can be accomplished by building
> partnerships between unlikely allies. We identify
> shared concerns, and we approach the farmer as
> a partner and ally in stewardship. Protecting the
> environment can be good for business, and in our
> experience the farmer is very invested in caring for
> their land.[39]

---

39 Ashley Boren. Interview by Lauren Speeth, July 7, 2012.

THE RIGHT PARTNER FOR THE RIGHT DANCE

Choosing partners carefully and not trying to make them something they are not is critical to success. Expecting academics to be practitioners, or vice versa, or expecting partners to veer from their core strengths can lead to failure. This was a challenge for us as Elfenworks got started, but we quickly learned to manage our expectations and choose our partners wisely to create a mutually beneficial relationship.

One of our earliest partnership efforts was creating a web based awareness-raising campaign, website, and logo for the Universal Health Care Action Network (UHCAN), a nation-wide network of disparate groups with different constituencies and approaches, united in their concern for health care justice. Partnership is mission-critical at UHCAN, and Director Rachel DeGolia offers the following partnership insight:

> Try to be perceptive about the strengths that others bring to the effort, whatever it is you are working on, because different individuals, different groups have diverse things to offer. Appreciating others for their strengths is the key to building relationships, coalition building, and getting things done. UHCAN plays a unity-building role in the health care justice movement and we often remind folks that we are all on the same side even when we differ on issues and strategies, and that it is vital that we appreciate and respect the different roles that different groups play. Work together whenever we can, and try not to get in each other's way when we cannot.

UNEQUAL POWER RELATIONSHIPS

Partnership has many nuances, both positive and negative, not the least of which is problems inherent in unequal power. Simply defined, power refers to the degree to which an individual or organization is able to make decisions.

An infant has little power. While he is able to exert influence through powerful lungs, often getting what he needs by screaming, he makes few decisions for himself. A child is given increasing opportunity to make decisions commensurate with her skills and maturity, but all options presented to her are acceptable to the parent. Maturity and financial independence create considerable decision-making opportunities.

Funding foundations, for example, often award grants to individuals and organizations that promote their interests. When working in partnership with fund recipients, the foundation is in a position of power. They must realize, however, that recipients, while committed to an honest exchange of information, might skew their data to ensure continuous funding. The foundation guards access to funding, while the recipient guards information. There is power inherent in the hoarding of either. At the very least, recognition of the unequal power relationship and a desire to work through issues can mitigate problems, if and when they arise.

Another area of unequal power that can affect partnership building is in the workplace. Author and Workplace Consultant Peter Block calls for a fundamental shift in the distribution of power, privilege, and purse strings, inviting readers of his book *Stewardship: Choosing Service Over Self-Interest* to let go of the belief that to care for something one must retain control, and to allow for a shared sense of ownership and vision.

Block also champions other ways to create balance in the workplace. He recommends managers empower the entire staff to participate as stakeholders in the hiring of new members, reducing secrecy as much as possible, and stressing partnership and shared vision. Seasoned managers may be interested in exploring this approach. However, just as with employers, worker perspectives can be flawed, systems can be abused, and if anyone fails to do his job at any time, work simply may stop. As Block acknowledges, workers "need to commit to act in the interests of the whole organization."[40] While individual needs and expectations must be acknowledged, individual agenda must be trumped by the needs of the organization, and decisions must be made accordingly.

---

40   Ibid., 67.

CHAPTER QUESTIONS

1. *How might happiness factor into a successful partnership?*

2. *What do you look for in a working partnership? List the five most important attributes in a partner organization. Why did you choose these over others?*

3. *Can you think of a time when you have made a questionable partnership choice? Did it work out? Why or why not?*

4. *Why is access to information or money an agent of power? Can you think of other examples?*

CHAPTER 7

PILLAR FIVE - CREDIT SHARING

Since its 1971establishment as a local coffee bean roaster in Seattle, Starbucks has become the largest coffeehouse company in the world. Some attribute the success to the company's ubiquitous presence; others claim customer service. And many cite the quality, consistency and diversity of the product for its popularity.

Yet marketing expert Mary Kaye Denning credits three other P's – Process, People and Profit. In terms of process, "Starbucks refers to its employees as partners," says Denning, president of the Manufacturing Mart in Cleveland, Ohio[41]. "While that may not mean that a barista will earn the same amount of money as the CEO, it does suggest that each employee is an integral element of the overall product." Employees can take pride in co-creating the company success, and participate in profit-sharing. Employee satisfaction rises, turnover falls, and the result is seen in the bottom line.

Pillar Five, Credit Sharing, is about being generous, gracious, giving. It makes good business sense; effective management credits contribution from subordinates and partners, and in return, reaps the rewards of pride, productivity, profit. Allowing others the opportunity to take credit means knowing how and when to acknowledge deserving partners, while having an ego mature enough to share the spotlight.

It also is good for the soul. Achievement, actualization and acknowledgement are so important to our human psyche that we crave credit, particularly when warranted, as a vital part of our sense of self

---

41   Mary Kaye Denning, "The Manufacturing Mart Promotes Plan for Job Shop Success and Employee Pride," (Cleveland, Ohio, July 2011), themanufacturingmart. com.

worth. This means developing consciousness around recognition is a critical element in managing and collaborating with staff.

Perhaps, on occasion, it means understanding or accepting that some will desire or receive credit that may not be warranted – and letting that go, as well. Our focus must remain trained on what matters.

REWARD FOR A JOB WELL DONE

Money is a powerful motivator. Although some say it can't buy happiness; most western societies have found it an essential tool in providing our food, clothing and shelter. According to Maslow's Hierarchy of Needs, a psychological theory Dr. Abraham Maslow introduced in his 1943 paper, "A Theory of Human Motivation," [42] our lives succeed to the extent that our needs are met, in a ranking order of importance to our survival.

Most fundamental is air, water, food, shelter, procreation and sleep. Once our basic needs are met, we seek the satisfaction of security regarding health, family, employment and property. At the next level, we look for love and belonging, friendship and intimacy, continuing up the hierarchy to the ultimate level of self-actualization. There we focus our attention on morality, critical thinking, creativity, achievement, acceptance and the chance to leave our legacy in the world.

Other than the air we breathe, our most basic needs are most often met through purchase. Even for the things we make for ourselves, we likely bought or bartered for materials. This is part of the reason or, in many cases, the only reason people seek employment, otherwise known as our livelihood or working for a living. Our employers allocate wages to compensate us for our skills and efforts, which we use to support our daily living. This is

---

42   Maslow, A.H. (1943). "A Theory of Human Motivation," *Psychological Review* 50(4): 370-96.

why receiving honest pay for honest work is essential.

Yet there is more to our merit than money. Those who work with us and for us also can benefit from less tangible forms of recognition which serve our higher-order needs: audience, accolade and acknowledgement. We want to be heard, to be appreciated and to be noticed, awarded, rewarded for a job well done.

THE CHANCE TO SHINE

When developing and implementing a new project, an established organization may choose to be subtle about the way they advertise their role, giving others a chance to shine. Rosanne Haggerty of Community Solutions notes on website 100khomes. org, "Our effort is beyond building an organization, it's about building a movement."

When I explain this Pillar to clients, I often point to The Carter Center's practice of naming projects. They named their Guinea worm eradication effort "Millennium 2000," using a generalized title to shift the focus from their organization and input, to the goal, so their partners could participate in the program's success.

Since 1986, The Center has been at the helm of the project to eradicate Guinea worm disease, a painful and debilitating disease caused by this waterborne parasite. A PBS special on March 18, 2010 reported a 99.9 percent success rate in eliminating the Guinea worm from the Americas and parts of Africa. These spectacular results put it on course to be the second human disease eliminated from the face of the earth, after smallpox, and the first to be eliminated with public health measures, without a vaccine.

At Elfenworks, we follow The Carter Center model, naming efforts generically, such as "Second Saturdays" and "The Butterfly Project." Every entrepreneur I interviewed for this book told me they view this Pillar as critical to their project's success. The Center for

Science in the Public Interest founder Dr. Mike Jacobson noted the important energizing effects of giving and receiving deserved credit:

> Sharing credit is important, both with staff and
> the outside world. Not disingenuously; that
> doesn't work. But getting deserved credit is really
> energizing, inspiring for people.

SHARED ORIGINATION

Social entrepreneurs who feel they have brilliant solutions may feel frustrated when they run into what seems like a "wasn't invented here" attitude. Sometimes others denigrate a program or idea if they didn't dream it up, themselves. Wise nonprofit directors generate ideas and participate in joint solutions, rather than imposing their own solutions on others – or rejecting ideas that were not theirs.

When I was interviewing Paul Minorini, President of Boys Hope Girls Hope, about the concept of giving others opportunity to take credit, he offered a keen insight about local development can foster a sense of ownership:

> What I have found over the years is that
> meaningful change, innovation and commitment/
> implementation of mission are most effective when
> they are inspired by great work, but "owned" by
> the individuals and groups trying to effectuate
> the change, innovation, or programs. I've seen it
> in our own work. For example, when we wanted
> to expand our services outside of residential
> programming in 2004, it didn't just come down to
> the affiliates as a mandate. Instead, we helped one
> affiliate develop and pilot test a solution. They took

ownership, and shared the model with others. We then used seed funding, working with each affiliate to find and refine an approach that would meet their community's specific needs. One key reason it was successful is that the change and innovation was seeded and inspired by a National vision, but developed and owned locally.

All of us need to feel we are making an impact. This need, which motivates us to be social entrepreneurs, isn't limited to us but also exists among our employees, our partners and those we serve. Recognizing this will go a long way toward creating valid partnerships and fostering real, meaningful change.

Consider what happens when we don't. Forget the contribution of an important ally, and you risk losing their support. Write a paper without crediting your sources, and it is called plagiarism, punishable by sullied reputation, academic sanction or law.

As President Carter has emphasized to me on various occasions, "There is no end to the amount you can get done, if you're willing to give away the credit." The question is: Are you in it for the glory, or to be an effective change agent? If you are truly committed to the outcome of your efforts and are truly able to work in a way that humbly shares the credit, you will enjoy the satisfaction of being an effective change agent more than seeing your name on a plaque.

According to this concept, effective change agents share the credit with integrity and graciousness, even among those who would take credit for someone else's sweat equity.

CHAPTER QUESTIONS

1. *Discuss: When have you been able to share the credit, and how did it feel?*

2. *What can happen when we don't share the credit for accomplishments? Have you ever experienced this? How did it feel?*

3. *List three examples of project names that were presented in this chapter, and discuss why they were held up as examples of sharing the credit – or not.*

4. *On a blank piece of paper, write your name in the center, and put the title "social entrepreneur" below your name. Surround your name with all the relationships you might be expected to have, in the role of social entrepreneur – employees, partners, clients, donors – and consider the way in which each might wish to feel ownership in a solution.*

CHAPTER 8

PILLAR SIX - FEEDBACK

In April 1985, the Coca-Cola Company launched a "new" *Coke*® formula with a "smoother, rounder, bolder flavor." Although the company reportedly had invested in two years of taste-test research, consumers balked. Not only that, they panicked, hoarding cases of "old" *Coke* and rejecting the new version on the shelves. Consumer's preference for the 100-year formula was undeniable. Within three months, and with a great deal of customer feedback demanding the *"real thing,"* the Coca-Cola company removed the "new" *Coke* and introduced *"Coke Classic*®*"* –a formula very similar to the original but sweetened with corn syrup and not sugar—in its place. We may never know whether what appeared to be a failure to obtain accurate customer preference feedback was actually a brilliant two-step strategy to introduce change to a formula about which consumers still feel very passionately.

Pillar Six, having a valid feedback loop, is perhaps the trickiest of them all. This is why I originally colored the pillar orange on my graphic; a color of warning. Just as threat levels of orange are meant to indicate high risk, if accurate and relevant feedback is not obtained, a social entrepreneur enters the battlefield unarmed.

In the business world, entrepreneurs must arm ourselves with information. Effectiveness is measured in various ways, including interest, appeal, public benefit, and R.O.I. (return on investment). In effecting change, you must understand what you expect as a return on your investment, how you will measure it, and what the information means.

Having a valid feedback loop means implementing scientific method in your work. This is not as hard as it may sound. It simply means you decide on the criteria by which you will call yourself a success before you begin a project, and then you measure the results along the way. The point is to make changes if the feedback you receive indicates that the results you are getting are not going to get you to the outcome you sought.

Measuring for results and making necessary course corrections are most effective in a healthy work and partnership environment. If a leader is unable to receive feedback, whether due to ego or fear, then staff is less likely to bring feedback that indicates trouble to the leader's attention. The leader sets the tone. A willingness to expose one's own failings and frailties creates a culture that allows for course correction.

In a foundation-grantee relationship, it can be difficult to obtain valid feedback from a grantee. This is because, from the point of view of grantee, frank feedback to the foundation about any weakness or failure can mean a cut in funding. To obtain valuable feedback from grantees, foundations may wish to write clauses into the funding documents that allow for both positive and negative results, or be actively involved in the project for which they desire accurate results.

MEASURE, MEASURE, MEASURE

Assessing program effectiveness involves repeated and relevant measurement. Yet one can always devise a rubric to yield desired outcomes, depending on who stands to gain from them. Motivation to draw certain conclusions is usually fostered by incentives. Since you get what you incentivize, you must take care not to create incentives for the wrong thing.

As an illustration of this point, the *Los Angeles Times* reported in February 2010 that some Georgia teachers—pressured to teach to the test and improve test scores—were erasing student test answers and correcting them.[43] Their incentive – a raise and increased classroom funding was sufficient incentive to motivate cheating. It also shifted them away from the higher purpose of adequately and authentically educating children.

WHAT METRICS, WHO PAYS? WHEN?

Assessment involves defining success, setting milestones, and comparing goals to outcomes. Understanding the First Pillar, Vision, means you already know what a successful outcome looks like, and you probably expect to see certain milestones along the way. Up front is the place to define your terms: the measure of success, the timeline, and milestones, in quantifiable statements, on paper. If outcomes do not meet expectations, assessment involves understanding why, and correcting the course if necessary. When outcomes are favorable, having proof of results – solid evidence of success – can help attract backers to your efforts, and even make a case for replication.

Many assessment tools are available to choose among. And looking at the best practices of others can help you clarify your best approach. Sometimes, measuring ROI (return on investment) makes sense, but not always, and not for choosing between apples and oranges. Comparing two separate projects in entirely unrelated fields can make one project look more worthy than another, when actually they are incomparable. Using just ROI, social entrepreneurs might tend to focus only on simple projects in third-world countries where the dollar goes further.

Just because something looks better on paper doesn't necessarily make it better. Sometimes, when looking at a return on investment, not all the benefits are captured and expressed. A prison

---

43 Richard Fausset, "Georgia Investigates Abnormal Test Scores," *Los Angeles Times*, February 17, 2010, http://articles.latimes.com/2010/feb/17/nation/la-na-georgia-scores17-2010feb17 (accessed May 28, 2010).

diversion project could have a hard time factoring in any local benefits (e.g., crime averted) and societal benefits (e.g., cost savings through avoiding incarceration, and improving tax base : tax-paying citizens rather than inmates). Notwithstanding the difficulty of pulling these factors into an equation on effectiveness, all of those factors do merit consideration in finding programs worthy of your support.

Sometimes, when circumstances permit, scientific method can be used, either in evaluating two groups within a target population or a target group before and after treatment. Sometimes it is possible to perform a meta analysis – combining data from multiple sources or studies – when evaluating a cluster of programs as a whole.

There is no one-size-fits-all metric. It is important to match the assessment with the project. It also is crucial that all stakeholders (investors, implementers) agree up front about the purpose of the program, the goal of the evaluation, what sort of assessment will be done, how much it will cost, how long it will take, when reporting will take place and who will bear the costs involved.

ASSESSING IMPACT AND CHANGING COURSE

Picture it. Five minutes before your PowerPoint presentation, your computer crashes. You call someone from the IT department, who immediately addresses the problem. You appreciate her efficiency. Just as quickly, she determines the computer needs a new part, which will take two days to order. For the purposes of your presentation, her support was not effective.

You may already understand that efficiency and effectiveness are two different things. For our purposes, efficiency refers to the extent to which time and effort are well invested, while effectiveness means actually getting something important done. While the former may lead to the latter, you need to bank on the latter. To be effective in your project, you need to understand on whom you want to have an impact, and whether you actually can give them what they need. Efficient isn't always effective. According to Rosanne Haggerty of Community Solutions,

> Impact means having a way of responding to what people need as opposed to just offering what you have. A lot of people get stuck defining their purpose as 'providing soup and sandwiches' when the recipients aren't actually hungry. So part of the work lies in helping social entrepreneurs move beyond what they know how to do to get closer to what people actually need them to do.

> This involves accurately assessing need; knowing enough about specific individuals to understand how to make a difference. Once you know who's suffering and what their needs are, that's when the alchemy of creativity and compassion begins, and your work becomes effective.

The ability to take in feedback and admit when the organization can do better is critical. Haggerty said she felt "chastened" by how comfortable her organization became doing things efficiently in a way they later learned could have been done more effectively. It takes vision to go back to the drawing board and ask, as she did, "What if just building houses isn't going to get us there?"

> What if what sustains us isn't satisfying their needs? What if we need to alter our vision to reflect theirs? What if we need to change our program, to shift or raise money to pay for what they truly need?

What if these buildings we're famous for creating
are just part of the answer, and what if people are
so taken with them that they think they're the only
answer?'

A healthy ability to accept and respond to feedback is useful in charting an effective course. Because of feedback, which inspired reflective thinking, Haggerty says, "We are challenging our own model, which I think is a really good thing."

Just because you start with a vision and a concept about where to go and how to get there doesn't mean you must follow that same path forever. Joyce Dattner, founder of the All Stars Project of the San Francisco Bay Area, states the case very well. "In some ways," she says, "it's been a 31-year experiment. And it continues to be an experiment. We've learned a lot along the way, created a performance based model for igniting and sustaining development and don't mistake that for 'We know what we are doing here.' In fact performance as a new method for seeing and creating possibility is our strength. We can experiment and continue to create new, innovative programs."

USING STATISTICS TO MOTIVATE PARTNERS

Metrics, or measures of quantitative assessment, can provide information helpful in motivating potential partners to work with you on issues you care about. If a potential partner makes a statement about their active involvement in an issue, and you see a way to move forward they are not yet embracing, metrics can help make the case.

If technical feedback can be useful in developing potential partnerships, imagine how helpful it can be with current partners who are not performing as well as might be hoped. Dr. Donald Hopkins, who directs The Carter Center's Guinea worm eradication effort, believes one must approach any problem by first articulating the problem, then showing a solution to that problem, and implementing the solution by providing leadership.

Sometimes, in Dr. Hopkins' experience, the problem is plagued by poor performance throughout an entire region, making strategic use of feedback data essential. To illustrate this point during a lecture on Guinea worm eradication efforts, he showed three slides he had created, entitled, "We Use Data to Inspire Competition," "We Use Data to Make the Right People Uncomfortable." My personal favorite was the "Guinea Worm Race," graph that colorfully depicted the countries where guinea worm remained. It showed them as contestants in a foot-race, with some well ahead of others. On the runners, he had placed small portraits of the leaders of countries where the Guinea worm remained. As he told his audience, his tactic was aimed at making the right people squirm in their seats, and inspire them to get busy with the important work of eradication.

ILLUSTRATION: GUINEA WORM RACE

Source: Dr. Donald Hopkins (creator of graph), The Carter Center. Power-Point Presentation on Guinea Worm Eradication, February 2010.

USING THE PRESS FOR FEEDBACK

Scientists, such as Dr. Mike Jacobson of the Center for Science in the Public Interest, are reportedly quite comfortable with the scientific method that involves data collection and review, measurement and course correction. So it might be surprising to learn that Dr. Jacobson feels his most important feedback mechanism is the media, with whom he has built a trust relationship throughout the many years he has worked in advocacy. He feels accurate reporting "tells us what people think of certain ideas."

> In general, our feedback loop is the media... We have a long record of integrity and accuracy. What we say is generally right, and we don't make many mistakes of judgment. When we're criticized, I don't automatically say, 'Let's change our course of action.' It may cause us to change our message or perhaps guide us in some way. Or, we may just continue saying what we're going to say. But we certainly listen to the feedback.

FEEDBACK FOR IMPACT

Many nonprofit organizations and many foundations publish reports of their impact, and others look at their publications when making donation decisions. Recognizing that such reports may have an impact on future fundraising can create a very real disincentive to reporting accurate impact or measuring the right achievement, unless a culture is cultivated that allows for failure along the road to success.

Gil Crawford, CEO of MicroVest, a for-profit entity that provides capital to financial institutions that serve the working poor, measures dollars lent to the bottom quartile, rather than trying to make statements about which of the micro loans have been "best" for the poor, or trying to only focus on the poorest of the poor.

> "We let market forces do their work, and simplify how we define success. The scaling we see in microfinance is due to laser-like attention to the measurement of profit, and the alignment of everyone's interests."

LACK OF FEEDBACK LOOP

Where a valid feedback loop is lacking, society suffers. Consider the treatment of mental illness in America. Insufficient feedback about the impact of policy has exacerbated problems in this arena.

When mentally ill patients were released from institutions beginning in the 1960s, the decision was made to save money, rather than invest in services that would support their successful integration in society. Without supportive services, they failed, and we now pay a high cost to institutionalize many of them in prisons, where they receive little or no mental health care. Rosalynn Carter calls this phenomenon "trans-institutionalization," a practice reminiscent of 16- and 17th-century customs.

Today, the cost of untreated mental illness – both to the individual and to society – is much higher than the cost of treatment. According to Carter, almost 60 million adults in the United States suffer from a diagnosable mental disorder in any given year, with 13 million of them suffering from the most serious forms of mental illness.[44] Yet untreated mental illness takes a high toll on both the individual and employer, with depression alone responsible for 400

---

44   Rosalynn Carter, Susan Golant, and Kathryn Cade, *Within Our Reach: Ending the Mental Health Crisis* (New York, NY: Rodale Press, 2010), 17.

million sick days a year.[45]

Rosalynn Carter calls the treatment of veterans, in particular, for whom the experience of trauma can bring on post-traumatic stress symptoms, a "national disgrace."[46] In addition, the elderly, already a stigmatized group, are doubly stigmatized when they suffer depression or any other mental illness, worsening health outcomes.[47]

It's important to compare apples to apples, when demonstrating impact. While costs for the humane treatment of the severely mentally ill might be high, they are minimal in comparison to the costs of incarceration. Fr. Peter Young, of his eponymous housing and treatment organization, brings a metric measurement to his impact, not only in averted costs, but in taxes generated by former clients who now contribute to society and experience the dignity of a paycheck.

Valid feedback about the actual costs and benefits to society helps policy makers and donors make smarter, investments and more humane decisions.

VISION IMPLEMENTATION SHIFTS

If you truly are open to feedback, then you are open to being changed by it. As you grow and change, feedback can have an impact on the way you operate in the world. As you recognize new skills, or new problems, or realize where your focus is best directed, the scope and nature of your activities will likely change as well.

At Elfenworks, the vision of "working for hope in America, one good thought at a time," has remained, but I have grown in my understanding of what that means, exactly, and also how to implement it successfully. At first, Elfenworks simply supported

---

45   Ibid.

46   Ibid., 91.

47   Ibid., 75.

others, with website work or film support. Then, collaborative efforts were added and, finally, we invested in internally originated projects.

MEASURING IMPACT DURING DOWNWARD TRENDS

It often is hard to measure the impact you are having. Sometimes, when you are working in an area where trends are worsening, you can feel as if you are measuring out cups of water from a sinking ship. It would be wonderful if we, like George Bailey in *It's a Wonderful Life*, could be given the gift of seeing our impact over a lifetime. In that movie, George, played by Jimmy Stewart, is at his wit's end and wishes he had never been born. An angel grants him the wish, and he sees the negative impact of his absence, on the world. Sometimes, we measure only the problems, without recognizing all the good we have done. It is good to keep in mind that your work could be the difference between sinking and drowning, to those on board your ship.

You don't have to be a numerical wizard or a statistical genius to measure the impact of your contribution; you can have help. But a lack of skill or experience is not a good excuse for not measuring what you are doing. Go get the skills, or hire them. Find a way to get the feedback you need. Having a valid feedback loop is critical to everyone who hopes to make a real difference.

CHAPTER QUESTIONS

1. Discuss: What are the dangers to the social entrepreneur in not having a valid feedback loop?

2. Name three barriers to appropriate and complete feedback. Discuss ways in which you, as a social entrepreneur, might lessen their occurrence.

3. Note one area in the public or private sector, in which you see appropriate and complete feedback as lacking. Do you see solutions? What are they?

4. On the center of a piece of paper, write your name as social entrepreneur. Around you, add the various people from whom you might be able to obtain feedback. Consider how often you request such feedback and how you might go about improving your feedback loop.

CHAPTER 9

PILLAR SEVEN - STAYING POWER

Joel Osteen, televangelist, author and senior pastor at Lakewood Church in Houston, Texas, frequently preaches the importance of "speaking faith" into others, into ourselves, into our efforts. By this, he means to put into words the belief and expectation that we have what it takes, that we can, even against all odds, prevail to realize our dreams.

One of his most frequent examples is the realization of the Compaq Center sports arena to become the house of worship for Lakewood Church. From 1975 to 1998, the facility, known as The Summit, served as a multi-purpose sports area, which housed various professional teams, and presented live concerts and other special events.

In 1998, Compaq computer technology firm bought the naming rights to the arena, which became the Compaq Center, until 2003, when the facility was leased to Lakewood Church. After seven years of renting in a 30-year lease, the Church requested to purchase the building. After three years of faith and struggle, the City Council approved the sale of the building to Lakewood Church.

Today, Pastor Joel Osteen preaches to a local audience of 16,000 at Lakewood Church, and reportedly another seven million broadcast viewers in some 100 countries. He credits his success to faith and to, against all odds, staying the course.

The final Pillar, Staying the Course for the Long-Term, is as critical as the First Pillar – the Vision that set you on your course. Staying power involves keeping faith in the vision over time, taking a realistic view of the road ahead, and developing the ability to be single-minded about the task at hand, without being sidetracked by distraction or disappointment. It means allowing for the inevitable bumps along the path and not letting them get in the way of your progress.

LONG-TERM VIEW

Just because you have done your homework and have found the vision that makes your heart sing, and just because you are using your special skills to make a difference in that area, doesn't mean you won't, at times, feel overwhelmed, have second thoughts or doubt your skills, abilities, support system or vision to see it through. Knowing that these bumps in the road are part of the journey might help you keep them in perspective when they arise. So will understanding what helps you, personally, when you hit a rut. And, when this happens, seek ways to renew your inspiration. Revisit your mission, take a break, try again – differently. I derive a great deal of pleasure from visiting the ocean and from bird watching. These activities fill me back up and renew my enthusiasm for my work.

POLICY IMPLICATIONS

Over time, and as you experience successes and setbacks, you may find that your vision evolves and you more clearly see a problem's root cause. Sometimes, this can inspire a new sense of hunger, drive, and determination for systemic changes. And sometimes, you may find yourself advocating for policy – courses and principles of action – at the local or national level, to address underlying root causes. Because such efforts can be met with resistance, you may find it prudent to become part of the system you are trying to influence, as many *In Harmony With Hope* award winners have done. For example, Fr. Greg Boyle is a consultant to the USDOJ National Gang Advisory Board, and Fr. Peter Young, who serves as chaplain for the N.Y. State Senate, founded the

Alcohol and Substance Abuse Treatment Program within the Department of Corrections.

Policy is a very different world from hands-on helping, requiring its own set of special skills. Not everyone is attracted to, or effective engaging with, policy issues.

REALISTIC VIEW

In *The Wizard of Oz*, Dorothy sets out with her newfound friends toward their respective visions. Skipping along, they follow the Yellow Brick Road, anticipating a smooth, straightforward path to Oz. Yet they are beset by twists, turns and traps along the way.

A more realistic view would be to understand that, while there may not be a "wicked witch" at every turn, there will be challenges and setbacks in any good and important work. Knowing this, and preparing yourself beforehand, may not make the challenges easier, but it will help you weather the journey, with the ultimate goal in mind as you stay the course.

DEALING WITH DISTRACTIONS

If your efforts already have brought you to the Seventh Pillar, you have been at your work for a while. You even may be at the point where you are getting some early results. Those results may be spectacular, disappointing or as yet unrealized. Undaunted, you press on.

Then, you turn on the news or receive a plea in the mail unrelated to the mission of your work, which interests you or pulls at your heart strings. Perhaps someone walks through your door with a smooth pitch. Somewhere in the back of your mind, you hear "Danger!" and yet that siren song calls to you. Part of you feels like surrendering because "Yes, I could help."

Consider yourself in treacherous waters, on the horn of a

dilemma, caught between Homer's mythical sea monsters Scylla and Charybdis. You have to choose between two evils: ignoring another potentially worthy cause or letting your main mission sink while you swim after something new. Consider that your main mission could capsize if you fall for the siren song. Tie yourself to your mast, and let the ship sail on through.

Not all missions are so divergent from yours as to be obvious distractions. It is easy to identify the distraction when you are working on saving whales and you receive a request to work on behalf of orphan children. But what about other, more similar causes that run the risk of redirecting your attention? What about the plight of the Manatee or the Polar Bear? Establish the scope of your work and stick to it. A good Board of Trustees can help you stay focused and on track, and keep your team from exhausting itself by working on an effort too broad to address.

THE BUMPS

Inevitably, challenges will arise while entering any arena in need of a social entrepreneur. Knowing in advance that mistakes are part of the process can help soften the disappointment of our initial failures along the road to our successes.

Understanding and applying the Seventh and final Pillar is critical. When we know in advance there will be speed bumps, we are more likely able to make corrections and stay the course. Particularly if we can anticipate them. They may be generated by conflicting perspectives, funding shortfalls, staff issues, misunderstandings or other common but frustrating shortfalls. Nevertheless, if we can keep the faith and the focus, while allowing for failures along the way, we are more likely to reach our destination.

VISUALIZATION

I still remember the moment when I was preparing for a difficult solo, and my violin teacher told me to "visualize the 'after party'" – to imagine celebrating with friends after a successful performance. I realized he was giving me a way, not only to get through the solo, but also to see myself doing it well, so I could create that reality. After trying it, I found I did indeed arrive, triumphantly, at the imagined moment; the "after party." This visualization technique works to bring all kinds of intentions to fruition; particularly, I have found, sustained effort in difficult areas.

Perhaps you already have had such moments. Maybe you, too, have been "on stage" before, just like the young violinist about to give a big solo performance. Or maybe it was a more personal moment, when you found yourself sitting at your desk, overwhelmed by the task at hand. Next time, shift your energy by visualizing your satisfaction at accomplishing your goal, knowing you have made a real, positive and lasting difference that has moved your heart. That visualization will grow closer to reality and, as you continue your work, it will provide you with strength courage, conviction and a way to see yourself there.

You also can use that "heart" feeling to give you insight in making decisions, as you ask yourself what the "after party" moment feel like with your project. The imagination is a powerful tool. If you can quiet your mind and concentrate on your vision of success, it can be truly transformative and help you achieve your goals.

SETBACKS AS STRENGTHENERS

Surely you have heard that old saw, "What doesn't kill you makes you stronger." I have never subscribed to it completely because sometimes it just isn't so. Poison, given in small doses, for example, can weaken and cripple. But there is a grain of truth to it.

Consider this: Two groups of people cross a river in two different rowboats. One group rows across still waters without much exertion, arriving easily, at the opposite shore. The other fights some stormy seas, yet works together in new and creative ways. They arrive a little more tired but more unified as a team and, because of what they have learned, better able to face whatever obstacles they may encounter on land. Of course, a third group, as the old joke says, wander up the shore a ways, discover a bridge, and walk easily across the river.

Identifying the opportunity in what seems like a setback; for example, seeing it as a team-building exercise or chance to explore, can help ease the pain of the setback, enabling you to regroup and move ahead toward your "safe shore."

SETBACKS AS FEEDBACK

There is no getting around it; when you try something and you fail, it hurts. Looking at the setback as a source of new, helpful information can help take some of the sting out of the setback.

Amy Hamlin, director of Volunteers in Medicine, says it is from her organization's failures that she has learned how to recognize whether a new clinic will or will not be successful. From her efforts in Detroit, she learned,

> There's certainly enough need, but there aren't
> enough resources there, either volunteer or
> financial, to sustain a clinic. When the government
> puts in an FQHC (Federally Qualified Health
> Center) and we pair a free clinic with an FQHC,
> we can get the lion's share of the uninsured into a
> community; we can succeed.

Why not look at setbacks not as failures, but as feedback, providing information that makes you stronger, more insightful going forward?

INDIFFERENCE AS A SETBACK

When we are excited about a project, it can be disappointing when our efforts aren't met by others with the same level of enthusiasm. Robert Egger, founder of DC Central Kitchen, noticed indifference to his determination to change the way we distribute food to the homeless. Yet he now feels DC Central Kitchen has struck a chord with people, who can understand the effective model of collecting food that would otherwise go to waste and providing it to the homeless being retrained as chefs.

Perhaps the Kitchen has served as a kind of elephant in the room, begging people by its very presence to talk about an uncomfortable subject they would rather not look at: poverty. It has inadvertently provided something people can latch onto, not unlike the house-building done by Habitat for Humanity; it captures the imagination, inspires the satisfaction inherent in team work.

Egger said, "Once people come and see what we do, the challenge is to guide the public toward that breakout moment, to talk about not just what we do at the Kitchen, but what the big WE, society, must do, to break the cycle of poverty and inequality."

PERSONAL SOURCES OF STRENGTH

I asked President Jimmy Carter[48] about staying the course for the long haul, as he has succeeded in doing. How would the Pillars methodology be helpful? Should "allowing for bumps" include balance, and cover mental, emotional, physical and spiritual components? Should it mention eating right, exercising, and

---

48   Jimmy Carter. Interview by Lauren Speeth, February 25, 2010.

observing the Ten Commandments, including keeping the Sabbath, in order to replenish one's self?

The pressures of work and family commitments make the commandment about a "day of rest" appear inconvenient if not impossible. Yet it is set out among Moses' top 10 edicts for a reason, as a remembrance of a deliverance from bondage, as well as a small deliverance from the bondage of our own making.

President Carter said these were all fine tenets, and that he takes Sunday off and also stops after a day's work and does not return to work until the early morning. He reports feeling fresher than if he had kept going all night. He also keeps hobbies and takes in the local flavor when he travels.

But this wasn't as important as a key element he stressed to me. "There's one you didn't mention," he said, "which is prayer. I've resorted to prayer several times a day if I faced a challenge. I aligned myself as best I can in my human, fallible way, with a partner who knows everything. It may be self-delusional, but it associates me with equanimity: some things I cannot change, and if I fail, the question is only did I do the best I could?"

To really stay the course for the long-term, in the face of obstacles, President Carter's answer is contemplative prayer. Maintaining a relationship with divine guidance can help order your steps and light your path, even when that path becomes shadowed by doubt or dilemma.

One Million Lights' Director Anna Sidana provided insight into the phenomenon of compassion fatigue, a readily recognizable barrier to staying the course in the nonprofit sector:

> Compassion fatigue results from giving without
> connecting with the cause; the people. Perhaps it is
> the people who are in a position to give who are so
> disconnected with themselves, society at large and

more fundamentally, nature, that they are not able
to get the healing one can get from simply giving.

In order to combat compassion fatigue, or donor burnout, Sidana suggests people find an emotional connection with their giving, and support what they are passionate about. Sidana is thinking generationally. She partners with local schools and also doctors, who raise funds to change the lives of children in the most remote regions.

Fr. Peter Young, who runs a critical rehabilitation, job training and housing program in the state of New York, introduced me to the concept of the *wounded healer*, one who has faced the same addiction or other traumatic experience yet has triumphed over his adversity. He believes those who have walked the same path, yet have entered the tunnel and emerged on the other side might have more staying power than others when counseling recovering addicts. Fueled by their own insights, experiences and empathy, they would be less likely to suffer from burnout and apathy than the average volunteer.

Fr. Young was taught the concept by Sr. Ignatia, whom he hails as one of the unsung founders of Alcoholics Anonymous. Wounded healers tend to find helping others who are still making their way along the path to recovery deeply fulfilling. He writes about why wounded healers are best:

> They have been there. They know what their
> clients are going through, and are able to develop
> a much greater empathy with their clients than
> a person who has no personal knowledge of the
> problem... [They] have a greater stake in the care
> of the clients; they tend to stay with it longer and
> most often do not develop the apathy that many
> other people develop over the years.

We use the system of wounded healers at every level of our treatment process, and we find it is one of the main reasons for our success... Our wounded healers are anything but apathetic. They love their work and stick with it. They continue to spread the work of recovery and enthusiasm.

DON'T DECLARE SUCCESS TOO EARLY

Dr. Donald Hopkins of The Carter Center warns the social entrepreneur: "Don't declare success too early. It is not over till it's over. In working to eradicate the Guinea worm, for example, the standard for declaring success in a country is that three years have to have passed without any cases. There has to be good monitoring, so if there had been a case, the likelihood is high we would know about it."[49]

Journalism students are taught about a very close presidential election race when a newspaper declared success too early – for the wrong candidate. Writers for the Chicago Tribune examined the polls, looking for a winner. Time was short, the press deadline was looming, and some of the more experienced reporters were on strike. Those on duty that night typeset the headline, "Dewey Defeats Truman." The paper declared the news early November 3, 1948, but it was wrong; Truman had won.

Half a century later, it happened again during another close race when broadcast news media reported that Vice President Al Gore had defeated George W. Bush in the 2000 presidential election. Although Gore reportedly was ahead by 500,000 popular votes, Bush lead Gore by four electoral votes. A surfacing of "voting irregularities" in Florida further exacerbated the confusion. Five

---

49   Dr. Donald Hopkins, "Carter Center Guinea Worm Eradication Effort Briefing," Port St. Lucie, Florida (February 24, 2010).

weeks passed before the outcome of the election was confirmed.

Similarly, I still remember when, as a child, I steered a toboggan down a steep hill with my father. Almost there, I declared, "I did it!" and proceeded to drive us into a tree, which gave up all its snow from its branches. My father said, "Did what?" My answer today would be, "I declared success too early."

How do you develop staying power to see the project through until success truly arrives, and you are truly ready to welcome it in? Keep a realistic view of the amount of work it will take to get something accomplished. Learn to anticipate setbacks and distractions, and be ready for them.

When the bumps come, seek to consider them growth opportunities. In addition, having a sense of calling, being suited to the work you do, keeping a prayerful practice and maintaining some life balance can help you avoid burnout and stay the course all the way across the finish line to success.

CHAPTER QUESTIONS

1. *Discuss: What mindset helps in preparation for bumps in the road?*

2. *What practices help you "allow for bumps"? What about physical wellness? Behavior? A weekly day of rest and restoration?*

3. *Discuss: Describe your own practices that help you stay the course. How might you improve your practices?*

4. *Recall a time when you or someone you know declared completion or success of their efforts too soon. What happened? What did you learn from the experience?*

CHAPTER 10

A PILLAR TOOL

It is an enlightened society that understands that knowledge is power. As the Roman philosopher Epictetus said so succinctly, "only the educated are free." Yet the functional society realizes the power of knowledge is realized in its application. It isn't just in having knowledge, but in using it that we become empowered.

While the concepts behind the Seven Pillars may take a little time to absorb, by now you should have a good understanding of their value and purpose. What you need next is a way to apply them. From the moment you conceptualize your vision, to time you implement your plan, you need to be constantly evaluating the effectiveness of your project. The Seven Pillars can be applied as a tool to help you rate or assess your progress. In this chapter, I'll show you how to use this tool.

ILLUSTRATION: PILLAR PROJECT RATING TOOL

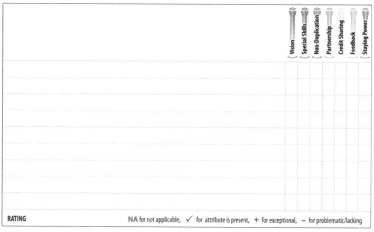

RATING   NA for not applicable, ✓ for attribute is present, + for exceptional, − for problematic/lacking

LEGEND
- Vision: unwavering vision, even in the face of challenges?
- Special Skills: Is this project taking good advantage of our special skill set?
- Non-Duplication: Is nobody else addressing this area effectively?
- Partnership: how well is this partnering with the stakeholders?
- Credit Sharing: are we doing this for the results, or the kudos?
- Feedback: do we have measurable deliverables and are we tracking them?
- Staying Power: how well can this project weather setbacks?

HOW THE TOOL WAS DEVELOPED

The Seven Pillars methodology has been in daily use at The Elfenworks Foundation since I explored its basic tenets with President Carter in 2006. In 2010, I decided to formalize the practice with a worksheet, to help all of us apply the methodology. Soon after, I made the worksheet available online, at The Elfenworks Foundation website, *http://elfenworks.org/creating-change*.

When I was developing the first prototype, I "test drove" it with my team at Elfenworks and with students at two California colleges: Mills College and Saint Mary's College. I used the classroom opportunity to invite both graduate and undergraduate students to try early versions of the worksheet and evaluate a potential Elfenworks Foundation project that was in the early exploration stage.

I then asked visionary nonprofit leaders I knew to offer their opinions and alternative formats, if they had any for me to consider. None gave me another framework, and many of them were complimentary of mine.

Rosanne Haggerty, founder of Common Ground and Community Solutions, later told me she has returned to the tool many times. "It's provided a helpful logic for some of the things we've been doing intuitively," she said. "It's a great language to share especially around how to make decisions."

Anna Sidana, founder of One Million Lights, said, "It provides a practical and yet insightful way to approach social entrepreneurship. These pillars offer common-sense thinking and guide you in your strategy, everyday functions and decisions as a leader."

Boys Hope Girls Hope executives, too, told me they planned to use the Seven Pillars framework; Bay Area Executive Director Suzanne Palmer said it can assist in her working toward achieving status as a regional center of excellence.

WHERE IT STANDS NOW

Now that the worksheet has been made available online, others have begun accessing and applying it. And the interest isn't limited to nonprofit organizations. Government agencies, too, are finding the worksheet valuable. The Chief Counsel for OSHPD, the State of California's Office of Statewide Health Planning and Development, Elizabeth C. Wied, Esq., utilizes the worksheet and methodology as a management tool. Further, interest isn't limited to the United States. According to Christopher Vas, former Assistant Director of the Department of Education, Employment and Workforce Relations, this tool is relevant to the Australian social policy context and will find interest even in the Australian Government.

USING THE TOOL: WHAT TO KEEP IN MIND

Perhaps the most important information regarding this tool is how to get started. Where should you jump in? The first step is to decide what you are interested in rating. This can be a future project or a potential grant recipient or an awardee. Here are a few ideas to consider as you evaluate your project, Pillar by Pillar:

- Vision: Is this project founded on vision? Does it have a basis for conviction? Are there naysayers, and is their objection relevant? Does this project fit within our vision?
- Special skills: Is the scope of the project within the special skill-set of the person or project group under consideration?
- Non-duplication: Is this a "me too" project, or is it based on filling a true need? You will need to do extensive research to know with certainty that the need is not already being met by another organization.
- Partnership: How well do project participants identify and partner with the true stakeholders?
- Credit sharing: Examine name selection, project purpose

and history. Is the individual or organization looking for results, kudos, or both?

- Feedback: How likely is it that valid feedback will be obtained? How open are channels of communication? Are criteria for success established? Can you develop a qualitative or quantitative analysis of the project's accomplishments?

- Long-term view: Can this project weather setbacks? Has it already done so? Is there a long-term viewpoint built into the project? Have the principal players been through other long-term projects? How likely is this project to survive?

PARTNER / AWARDEE SELECTION

The Seven Pillar worksheet easily can be used to rate other organizations, either when selecting between partners or among potential awardees, for awards or grants. The first step involves locating and making a list of potential partners or awardees. The next step is to rate them according to each of the Seven Pillar criteria. As an example, for the first Pillar, vision, consider whether the group shows vision even in the face of challenges and whether their vision, overall, is in line with your own.

RATING PAST EFFORTS

Perhaps you have completed many projects. It could be that some of these have not been fully analyzed for effectiveness. Knowing what has worked and what hasn't, and where we have been most effective, helps us to focus our best efforts in the future.

When I developed this worksheet, we at Elfenworks had many concurrent projects, as well as many completed projects, which had never been fully evaluated by our team, an important step in assessing the effectiveness of our work and the projects we support. So, we used the grid to rate them. Taking s good, clear look at ourselves was a turning point at Elfenworks. It helped us to understand ourselves, and to do a better job selecting and supporting projects.

Here is the result in a list of projects, with a compilation of staff ratings, Pillar by Pillar:

EXAMPLE – RATING HISTORIC PROJECTS

TEF Historic Projects	Vision	Special Skills	Non-Duplication	Partnership	Credit Sharing	Feedback	Staying Power
UHCAN	NA	+	−	✓	✓	✓	NA
INEQUALITY.COM	✓	✓	+	✓	✓	+	+
CVP.UCSF.ORG	✓	+	+	+	✓	✓	✓
IN HARMONY WITH HOPE ℠	NA	+	+	+	✓	✓	✓
ELFEN WORKS AWARD	NA	+	−	NA	✓	✓	NA
ART AS ACTIVISM MEDIA	+	+	+	+	+	+	+
PUBLIC AWARENESS CAMPAIGNS	+	✓	+	✓	+	+	+
PARTNERSHIP: CMF	NA	+	+	+	+	+	✓
PARTNERSHIPS: ACADEMIC	✓	✓	+/−	✓	+/−	+/−	✓

RATING NA for not applicable, ✓ for attribute is present, + for exceptional, − for problematic/lacking

LEGEND
- Vision: unwavering vision, even in the face of challenges?
- Special Skills: Is this project taking good advantage of our special skill set?
- Non-Duplication: Is nobody else addressing this area effectively?
- Partnership: how well is this partnering with the stakeholders?
- Credit Sharing: are we doing this for the results, or the kudos?
- Feedback: do we have measurable deliverables and are we tracking them?
- Staying Power: how well can this project weather setbacks?

SELECTING AMONG FUTURE EFFORTS

Often, there is more work than realistically can be accomplished. Hard choices need to be made. The worksheet can help in making these choices. To use the worksheet to help cull projects, the first step involves thinking through which future projects seem most viable, and writing them down on a Future Efforts list. Then, evaluate each project according to the Pillars.

Pillar One: Vision. How well does this project plan fit within our overall vision? If this is a collaborative project, how well do partner vision(s) align with our own? Some projects will stand out as important and worthy of time, attention and resources. Others will pale by comparison, clearly demonstrating themselves to be less important, given the selection criteria.

Pillar Two: Special Skills. Relative to the project as you and your partners have defined it, are the individuals or organizations involved posessed of the appropriate skill set essential to moving the project forward toward completion? To answer the question, consider the skills required for the project, and whether the project plays to your core strengths, or those of your partners. Although there will be much to learn along the way, do you feel the project is a good match in this area? Finally, what key strengths necessary for project success are missing, and how might you address this lack?

Pillar Three: Non-Duplication. What kind of research has been completed to ensure that the vision, the plan, and the projected results of this project are not already being realized effectively by others? Have participants identified a niche in which they can make a difference, or is the field saturated with work you simply have not yet identified how to do better?

Pillar Four: Partnership. Working with people who understand and share your vision is essential to a mutually successful outcome. It is important to recognize that partnerships manifest in various forms, whether their contributions are financial, managerial, consultant, promotional, functional or in kind. Yet there must be a balance of power that includes a code of ethical operations, based on honesty, integrity and transparency.

Pillar Five: Credit Sharing. One of the quickest ways to earn or lose loyalty to a person or project regards giving credit where credit is due. Most people appreciate reognition for their efforts or achievements. It is the wise leader who understands how to build ateam and incentivize by sharing the credit for work done well.

Pillar Six: Feedback Loop. Just as Socrates believed "the unexamined life is not worth living," he also may have understood that the unexamined project is not worth implementing. Or, at least we have no way of knowing if it is or not. Without qualitative and quanitative systems of evaluation, we have no way of assessing the effectiveness of our efforts, no way of determining why our project is or is not working, no way of measuring the impact of our efforts, of recognizing our success. The project must have systems through which to obtain, interpret, accept or reject and apply feedback.

Pillar Seven: Long-Term View. Rarely is a project envisioned, strategized, implemented and developed without a series of switchbacks dogging the uphill climb. Every twist and turn, every speedbump along the path is merely an opportunity to reevaluate, regroup and improve the process. As columnist Arianna Huffington said in a graduation address, "Perseverance is the difference between success and failure. Failture is not the opposite of success. It's a stepping-stone to success.[50]"

EXAMPLE: FIRST STEP – LISTING THE PROJECTS

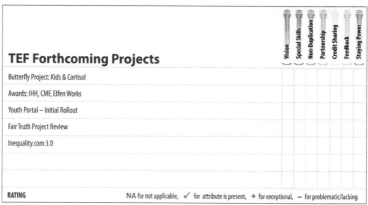

50   Marc Ferris. "Arianna Huffington Delivers Keynote Speech at Sarah Lawrence Commencement Ceremony" New Rochelle Patch. New Rochelle, NY: May, 2011.

FOR FEEDBACK CRITERIA: FUTURE EFFORTS

Using your "future effort" list, go across to the columns of attributes for each of the entries, and discuss the criteria you would use to rate them, relative to each other, by what means you would use to measure success or failure, and what the cutoff values are. This is a critically important point because without such criteria, you may be prone to subjective, post-hoc or after-the-fact evaluation.

CHAPTER QUESTIONS

1. *Consider and discuss why knowledge applied is essential to empowered work.*

2. *Discuss three possible uses for the Pillars as tools.*

3. *Choose one use (e.g., rating past projects) and complete a Pillar worksheet for your organization or a hypothetical organization. Discuss its practical application.*

4. *Consider how Pillar One, "Vision," can be rated, and the impact it can have on partnership. Next, choose another Pillar and discuss similarly, until you have thought through the application of all Seven Pillars.*

CHAPTER 11 - EPILOGUE

WHERE, FROM HERE?

Here are the stories of Gemma Rice, Jenn Adams and Bill Milliken, change-makers with very different visions. Rice and Adams work on behalf of children in Tanzania. Milliken, founder of Communities In Schools, is making a difference for children in the United States of America.

All his life, Bill Milliken, founder of Communities In Schools, struggled with an undiagnosed learning disability. Believing he was dumb, he saw no meaningful future, so he had—and caused—a lot of trouble in high school, and spent much of his time hanging out on the streets. Although he did graduate, his future wasn't looking bright. A chance encounter with a caring adult, a mentor, taught him to believe in a different life story, and changed Milliken's life forever. At the age of 20, he began working with homeless and addicted youth on the streets of Harlem and the Lower East Side of New York City; within a few years, he and a friend had founded 18 alternative schools they called "street academies," which featured coordinated community services to address the students' needs. Over the next 40 years, his work evolved into what is now the country's largest dropout prevention program, Communities In Schools. Bill has served under three U.S. presidents, including Jimmy Carter, for whom he was White House Advisor on Youth Issues. The program he founded is based on his first-hand experience understanding that programs don't change children, relationships do.

Consider Jenn Adams. Every time she takes a warm shower, drinks a glass of cool, clear water, washes her car, her dishes, her laundry, her face, Jenn thinks about the children who live without clean water. This 28-year-old, aqua-eyed blonde woman from

California had left her beach-front home and set out to a place she had never seen, to fulfill a lifelong dream to do international relief work in Africa. She soon found herself in Arusha, Tanzania, where another young woman, Gemma Rice, had left her home on a sheep farm in Australia to open the School of St. Jude in East Africa, to serve 1,500 of Arusha's poorest children.

These young women had grown up in relative comfort. Relative to Tanzania, and to much of the rest of the world, it might be considered exceptional comfort. But many who grow up warm and safe—who don't grow up wanting—always seem to want more. It's all relative. But something in each of them ignited a desire to help.

Then, when Jenn Adams saw the mud huts, the meager meals, and the dirty water—the primary cause of sickness and absenteeism—she became impassioned to go beyond what was expected of her at the school, and to change the situation for these children. In 2009, she returned to California to figure out how to de-worm these children that they might avoid parasitic diseases. After six months of research, she understood that medicine is no more than a Band-Aid unless there is clean water, sufficient sanitation, and health education. Water is life; choosing the name "Maisha," a word which means life in Swahili, she returned to Tanzania the following May to launch a pilot program. [51]

People don't often wake up with a plan in place for how they can have a positive impact on the world. It begins with an inspiration, an idea that awakens from an experience or event in their lives that ignites desire – passion, even – to make a change.

The caring adult who changed the trajectory of Bill Milliken's life certainly never imagined that this kindness would ultimately ripple out and benefit so many others. Likewise, Gemma Rice

---

51 Lisa Crawford Watson, "The Maisha Project: Woman's Project Pushes for Clean Water," Monterey County Herald, Monterey, CA (June 17, 2011).

could not have known that, by founding her school, she would not only educate children, but inspire a new organization to address clean water. The ripple effects from being a positive force in the world can amaze and surprise.

WHY NOT YOU?

A few years ago, I decided I wanted to grow blueberries. Blueberries aren't generally a crop for California gardeners; they're more often found growing in bogs in the East Coast. But blueberries have been my favorite fruit ever since my grandmother fed me blueberries with cream as a young child, and I really wanted to try to grow my own.

The first year yielded nothing. The second year had a few berries, but the birds ate them. The bushes weren't pretty, and I was considering giving up. I decided to add netting, and give them one more year. This decision didn't come easily for me; I'm not patient, and I like my garden looking pristine. The following year, I was rewarded with a bowl full of blueberries. I proudly emailed a photo of the bounty to my family, most of whom live on the East Coast.

Blueberries from the Garden

One of my sisters, who has been growing blueberries for years, reminded me, "there are late blooming and early blooming, high bush and low bush, so NEVER GIVE UP ON THE BLUEBERRIES!" Couldn't the same thing be said of your aspirations?

With total commitment, I have found it is possible to really be effective using the Seven Pillar methodology. If you are with me so far, you likely have found value in their premise and potential application. Yet while this entire book has been devoted to explaining and making a case for them, interpretation or application of the Seven Pillars still may raise questions. Sometimes, if we look at our reasons for rejecting something, we can demystify any fears or concerns.

TOO NEW?

The Seven Pillars is a relatively new framework for affecting change. This is the first published book about it, and reading about it is only the first step to utilizing this methodology. Many people would rather stick with what they know. Until the Seven Pillars gains a documented following, only early adopters will be compelled by it.

TOO SIMPLE?

The methodology is simple, and many people don't gravitate to simple. Gil Crawford, CEO of MicroVest, said, "I rarely see a business model that can be explained on a 3x5 card, but I can put the model of a well-run microfinance bank on a 3x5 card." Certainly we can print the Seven Pillar model on a 3x5 card. What is your position on methodologies that are simple enough to fit on a reference card?

FEAR OF GOING OUT ON A LIMB?

The first and last of the Seven Pillars stress vision, and the bumps in the road we may encounter en route to implementing our vision over the long-term. Sometimes, the very concepts and projects that evidence great vision are also those with a greater risk of failure. Their import can be overshadowed by the incentive to stay safe. It can be daunting to consider taking meaningful risks for the sake of implementing a vision for change. It also can be exciting and, in some cases, essential.

Crawford notes that foundations are like many commercial bankers, reluctant to take risk:

> They operate...unwilling to take risk. The
> people they are funding are [at the helm of]
> nonprofits. Because they operate in a world of
> limited resources, they tend to come to the same
> conclusions... In the for-profit world, we expect a
> few failures. Not so, the nonprofit world. There is
> no upside for a foundation or government to take
> risk. We need to create venture philanthropists who
> are rewarded or penalized based on measurable
> objectives.

Gary Oppenheimer, founder of AmpleHarvest.org, a nationwide campaign to enable home gardeners to share some of their harvest with food pantries, agrees[52]:

> We've been in an ongoing struggle to get the
> support AmpleHarvest.org needs to fully reach
> its potential of making food recovery as much
> the "norm" as trash recycling is today. America's

---

problem is not a lack of food. It is a lack of awareness of the healthy food we already have. AmpleHarvest.org has a solution, but funders are so removed from the idea that I regularly hear "we absolutely love what you are doing, but we've never seen anything quite like it so we can't help you. Keep it up!"

AmpleHarvest.org needs a full time staff of 5 to 6 people to do its work. Last week, I figured out that our annual budget represents only about 5 hours of the nation's leading domestic hunger-relief charity's annual budget. The problem has been that funders are looking to truck food across the country time and time again. We instead move information.

Funders continue to call the current approach to hunger in America a "solution" because it is all they've seen despite the fact that if it were really a solution, the problem would have been solved by now. In short, people are afraid to risk success.

When I was working in the area of international funds transfer at a major bank in the early 1980s, I experienced first-hand the adage "nobody ever got fired for going IBM." Our software ran on DEC minicomputers, and any time we would install something new, we'd need to explain why we weren't using the choice they perceived as safe. Although I am risk averse by nature, I now am willing to take risks on projects I believe in. Still, I can see how others, who are risk averse, could find risk-taking problematic or, at least, scary.

OVER-INVESTMENT IN SELF?

One source of hesitation can be the real, honest fear of failure. When we fail, it can damage our self-perception. And if we've been successful in other areas, perhaps in the for-profit world, we may be disappointed when we are not immediately successful in the nonprofit world, even though it realistically takes years to understand the nonprofit landscape.

There is another concern, about which founders should be aware even before beginning their work: Founder's Syndrome. This occurs when an organization has outgrown its founder. Maladaptive organizational behavior can affect decision-making and hiring. The insightful founder will think through succession from the organization's inception. Otherwise, as Crawford said, "The nonprofit founders have no incentive to let go of what they created. They have no equity, no golden parachute and no capital to leave with and create another entity."

OVER-INVESTMENT IN STATUS QUO?

People who are invested in the status quo can be considered stakeholders in a negative sense. Harvard law professor Jon Hanson's theory of deep capture delves into why dispersed costs and concentrated benefits can make it difficult for the social entrepreneur to counteract entrenched interests.[53] Society, he says, doesn't incentivize bold risk-taking on behalf of the marginalized, with possibility of failure. The status quo may, in fact, feel quite comfortable. And since change can be scary; sometimes we or our partners may want to stick with the "devil we know" rather than venture out into new territory. Resistance may arise.

---

53   See Jon D. Hanson, http://www.law.harvard.edu/faculty/directory/index. html?id=25, which points to http://www.lawandmind.com/ (accessed December 28, 2011).

With some enlightened thinking, we can look beyond society's risk/reward incentives to a greater good and the reward that will bring.

WHY IT WORKS

This book is less about the specific steps you will take to address, mitigate or solve your particular social issue, and more about the cognitive and spirit-based path you must follow to reach an understanding of what it means to be a social entrepreneur and how to see yourself in that context. Only then will you be adequately prepared to invest yourself in making a positive and lasting impact.

Of all the concepts you may glean from this writing, if you come to understand who you are and what you can become in this endeavor, I have given you what you need and deserve to be successful in realizing your vision.

By now, you have grown sufficiently familiar with the Seven Pillar methodology to make your own decisions about its value. If you have worked through the chapter questions, you may have the added benefit of also knowing yourself better. Either way, you probably have begun considering your own skills and talents and the issues that help clarify your vision.

By outfitting your "toolbox for change" with the methodology of the Seven Pillars, I have tried to provide you the concepts and tools I was looking for when I began to work seriously as a social entrepreneur. The project you will build upon these pillars is up to you.

Many stakeholders stand to benefit from empowered social entrepreneurs like you: Community developers struggling against entrenched interests, a community that needs good food, clean water, waste management, housing, sustainable seafood, agriculture, livestock; after -school enrichment programs, access to healthcare, substance abuse recovery, education, training, employment, hope.

Anyone who has an interest in being effectively uplifted is a stakeholder who stands to benefit from social entrepreneurs who embrace the Seven Pillar methodology: The blind, the hungry, the homeless, the mentally ill, the uninsured, the disabled veterans; teens who have taken to the streets; children aging out of foster care; former gang members; the formerly imprisoned; and anyone who is suffering the consequences of having made a mistake. These are among the members of society who could become marginalized or who may need help to get back on track. Who inspires you?

The generalized society has a stake in the work of the social entrepreneur, as well. All of us, rich and poor , will benefit when society becomes more just through the effective action of the empowered, intelligent, compassionate social entrepreneur. It is up to you to take it from here. So become empowered, be blessed, and make lasting and effective change for the greater good.

CHAPTER QUESTIONS

1. *Consider: Am I an early adopter, or do I prefer tried-and-true methods of social action?*

2. *Consider: What is my comfort level with risk when implementing a vision?*

3. *Discuss: Am I inclined to use the Seven Pillars? Will I use it formally or informally? Why? How might I improve on it, if I do intend to use it?*

4. *Consider: Name someone who would not be inclined to try the methodology. What would keep them from using it?*

SUPPLEMENTAL ESSAYS

Note, while these essays are offered as a supplement only, and not intended as a Hebrew or Greek reference, the author strives for accuracy. If you notice any errors, please contact the publisher, so that subsequent revisions may be corrected. Thank you for your help!

ESSAY SET 1: GREAT TEACHINGS

One of the most intriguing aspects of President Carter's Seven Pillar methodology is that, while he is a Christian and has developed a system congruent to the values of a lifetime follower of Jesus, this system is not expressly religious in nature. Thus, the Seven Pillar methodology could work well when grounded in other positive religious, ethical, and moral systems. Throughout this essay, I will touch on Buddhist, Islamic, Jewish and Christian teachings regarding charitable work and social action.

Our Greco-Roman Society

We are all taught, through religious, moral and ethical teachings, to care for others. Many of us remember the "Golden Rule" of doing unto others as we would have done unto us. But our present-day society, focused on a more materialistic, "me"-based culture, is at odds with these teachings. "Get ahead, or at least keep up at any cost," or worse, "Do unto others before they do unto me," is the none-too-subtle message we hear in the media we consume daily. There is no need to feel guilty; if there is any fault, we're told it lies with those who fall behind.

Today's Western culture isn't an Abrahamic culture. It is Greco-Roman. And the tendency to judge and marginalize others can be traced directly back to Greco-Roman Stoicism. In a nutshell, "We cannot know anything about the minds of the gods, so we should just accept what the fates deal to us as our lot in life." Greco-Roman culture gave us a lot of great things, including logic. We owe our logical thinking about success to the Greco-Roman culture as well: If success is but a matter of ability and hard work, a simple formula of talent plus hard work should always equal success. By this post hoc logic, when people don't succeed, it makes logical sense to blame them, right? But when we do so, we disregard restrictive social structures and stigmas, economic forces, ineffective or absent parents, lousy schools, disabilities, and bad luck. Further, when we use these lines of thinking, we disregard the teachings of the Abrahamic religions – Judaism, Christianity and Islam – as well as other spiritual and religious disciplines, including Buddhism.

A BUDDHIST BASIS FOR SOCIAL ACTION

India had a deeply entrenched caste system when Prince Siddhartha Gautama (563-483BC) was born. He became disillusioned with the country's caste system, noticing that nobody escapes aging, illness and death, and he rejected his splendid princely life, nearly dying from self-mortification in his search for an answer to the question of suffering.

Near death, under a Bodhi tree in Bihar, India, he finally decided to accept food, and sat in meditation until he understood and began teaching what he described as the Four Noble Truths and the Noble Eightfold Path to enlightenment. The Buddha's truths are: Life means suffering; the origin of suffering is attachment; cessation of suffering is attainable; and there is a path to that cessation. The Buddhist Path involves wisdom, ethical conduct, and development of the mind: 1) right view, 2) right intention, 3) right speech, 4) right action, 5) right livelihood, 6) right effort, 7) right mindfulness, and 8) right concentration. Some Buddhist schools speak of the three poisons of greed, hatred, and delusion which, with work, can be transformed into detachment, compassion and wisdom.

Buddhists see all suffering as arising from these three poisons. By following a Buddhist path and developing skills, including meditation and practice, compassion and wisdom can arise in place of this suffering.

Perhaps the Buddhist teacher best known in the west hails from Tibet: the Dalai Lama. In *An Open Heart; Practicing Compassion in Everyday Life*, his words echo those of Jesus. "May the poor find wealth, those weak with sorrow find joy. May the forlorn find new hope, constant happiness and prosperity. May the frightened cease to be afraid, and those bound be free. May the weak find power, and may their hearts join in friendship."[54]

One of the Dalai Lama's favorite prayers goes as follows: "So long as space remains, so long as sentient beings remain, I will remain, in order to help, in order to serve, in order to make my own contribution." With that prayer, which brings strength, confidence, and a sense of purpose, he is explaining the Buddhist practice of "Metta" – to wish for all beings to be happy and free of suffering. Jesus taught this very same practice, using different language.

The Dalai Lama is working to build bridges among Christians, Muslims and all people of good conscience, while showing them how important it is that we have a compassionate heart as part of our human society. He stresses over and over that he is a human being like everyone else, and we all have the same potential to create community. For him, spiritual growth need not be based on religious faith, but also can be grounded in secular ethics if we remember how interdependent and intertwined the web of life really is.

"When we resist indulging in a self-centered view of the world, we can replace it with a world view that takes every living

---

54 His Holiness the Dalai Lama, *An Open Heart: Practicing Compassion in Every-day Life* (New York, NY: Bay Back Books, 2002), 25.

being into account... Our compassion for others can grow as our recognition of their suffering does."[55]

The Dalai Lama's discussion of cultivating equanimity is like Jesus' call to love everyone, including our enemies. Both would agree that it is irrational to respond to injustice with hostility since that wouldn't hurt our enemies, only ourselves. Holding onto resentment is like taking poison and expecting someone else to die. Friends and enemies are defined by our attitudes. If we want to be well, the Dalai Lama advises that we need to be careful about the attitudes we hold in our hearts, and cultivate equanimity, a kind of mental composure, even under difficult conditions.

When the Dalai Lama was asked whether becoming more compassionate would be cause someone to do poorly in the working world, he answered that this question arose from ignorance regarding true compassion, because a larger view of compassion includes empathy for the aggressor, who ultimately will be harmed if allowed to take unfair advantage.[56] Compassion involves living in harmony and cultivating a just and fair sense of peaceful interaction.

A Buddhist social entrepreneur could readily apply his or her grounding in the noble Eightfold Path to the Seven Pillars, particularly the first: Vision. This is because the path gives rise to wisdom, ethical conduct and mental development. To Buddhists, only with such wisdom and mental development – right view, right intention, right effort, right mindfulness, right concentration – can delusion be avoided, and only with ethical conduct – right speech, right action, and right livelihood – will it be well carried out.

Similarly, the Buddhist social entrepreneur would be grounded in Pillar Two: Using Your Special Skills, because of to the Buddhist wisdom that arises from right view, the ethical conduct that arises

---

55 Ibid., 93.
56 The Dalai Lama, address at Maples Pavilion, Stanford California, October 14, 2010.

from right action and livelihood, and the mental development that result from right effort, mindfulness and concentration.

Pillar Three: Non-duplication finds its relevance in becoming centered, focused enough on our purpose, our vision, our goal, that we become well aware of anyone already implementing our project – or we understand it is our responsibility to carry out.

Pillars Four and Five: Working in true partnership and giving others the opportunity to take credit are a reflection of ethical conduct, which arises from right speech, right action and right livelihood. They also are grounded in the wisdom that arises from knowing that more can be achieved when others are validated, and the greater good is thus served.

Pillar Six: Feedback – measuring for course correction - requires wisdom and attention, which arises from right view. This means the ability to see things as they are. This guides the practitioner's actions (right action) in taking true measurements with right effort, and commitment to self-improvement with right intention.

Finally, the Seventh Pillar allows for bumps along a path, long-term. The Buddhist path recognizes the transient nature of the material world, and works, over a lifetime, to awaken the compassionate heart. So the long-term view is enfolded within the Buddhist practice, and all seven Pillars fit within the framework of the Buddhist Eightfold Path.

AN ISLAMIC BASIS FOR SOCIAL ACTION

The youngest of the Abrahamic religions, Islam promotes two forms of charity: Sadaquah and Zakah. The first, Sadaquah, just like Tzedakah in Judaism – a Hebrew word meaning "righteousness" yet often referenced as charity – is voluntary and a means of moral growth. The word has a root, *sidq*, which means truth. That the words are similar should not surprise; the Abrahamic religions arise from the same region. Sadaquah is deeply stressed in Islam, not only because of its importance in society, but as a means of spiritual growth for the giver.

The great charitable deeds emphasized by the Qur'an – the central religious text of Islam – include feeding the poor (69:33-34; 90:11-16; 107:1-3), assisting orphans (17:34; 76:8; 89:17; 90:15; 93:9, 107:1-2), and emancipating slaves (90:13; 2:177). Small acts are emphasized as well, and charity, including smaller acts of kindness known as Ihsan (doing good), should be central to Muslim practice. Nobody and nothing should stand outside this circle of compassion. The Qur'an advises charity not only to all humankind regardless of religion (2:271-4) but also to all creation (51:19).

The second form of charity, Zakah, (meaning growth or purification), is a compulsory giving (17:26). Conventionally set at 2.5 percent of annual savings (or savings held during 12 months), Zakah is collected to benefit the poor, debtors, wayfarers, collectors of Zakah, those held in captivity, and for "the cause of Allah" – loosely interpreted as general welfare. The value of the home is exempt, as are cars, clothes, personal use items and, according to many jurists, jewelry that has been worn.

Certainly there is much more to understand about the Islamic faith tradition as a basis for social action; we have focused here only on its concepts of charity.

A JEWISH BASIS FOR SOCIAL ACTION

Jewish beliefs and practices vary widely but are based largely on an understanding arising from certain writings, foremost being the Torah (the first five books of Moses). The Torah, the Prophets (*Nevi'im*), and the Writings (*Ketuvim*) are together referred to as *TaNaKh*. Each has been transcribed in Hebrew exactly, mistakes and all, from generation to generation, for many thousands of years. In addition, a tradition of commentary and interpretation exists in the Talmud and Midrash interpretation of Jewish texts. The investigation continues as one interpretation of Torah is that it will contain the answers the seeker needs when looking with an enlightened heart. *T'Orah* literally means "full of light."

Tradition holds that Moses wrote the first five books, or Torah, in 1200 BCE, beginning by looking at creation itself.[57] Torah begins with the story of Genesis, "Within the midst of the beginning, the *Source of Powers* hollowed out the heavens/firewaters (*aish* = fire, *mayim* = waters) and the earth." *Or, in Hebrew: Breishit bara Elohim et ha-shamayim v'et ha-aretz* (בְּרֵאשִׁית בָּרָא אֱלֹהִים אֵת הַשָּׁמַיִם וְאֵת הָאָרֶץ׃).[58] During the course of creation, God proceeded to separate light from darkness, fill the ocean and populate the land with living creatures. This description, while colorful, is not inconsistent with a big bang, a hot and dense explosion after which there was a cooling and separation into matter.

On the sixth "day," when humans arrived,[59] they were granted dominion over the rest of the creation. They also were given the responsibility to care for it.[60] In this passage lies the basis for social action, in the realm of sustainability and stewardship.

The Torah is filled with unsolvable statements, Escheresque buildings – artist M.C. Escher's study in relativity and infinity – and hidden numbers and puzzles. These may keep the busy brain in check, in order to better allow the heart to see the soul of the soul. It cannot be fully translated into English without some of the

---

57 Jhos Singer, in his lecture, "Divine Paradox: Judaism 101" San Mateo, CA: Congregational Church of San Mateo, August 29, 2009, translates Genesis as "within the midst of the beginning, the *Source of Powers* hollowed out the heavens/firewaters and the earth." He then goes on to point out parallels with what science now knows about the beginnings of the universe.

58 Ibid.

59 Genesis 2 Bereshit (בְּרֵאשִׁית)

60 Genesis 2.15

meanings getting lost. For example, the Hebrew word for *fear* is yirah (יראה), which is spelled exactly the same as the Hebrew word for *seeing* (ראה).[61]

IMPERFECT LEADERS

Another good lesson from the Torah reveals how many flawed leaders there are. You don't have to be perfect, it seems to say, in order to bring about real and lasting change. Noah got drunk; Jonah ran away from the call until the undeniable intervention of a whale, and Moses murdered an Egyptian and fled into the desert before being called on by God.

SPIRITUAL STORIES AND STEWARDSHIP

Even though many depths and nuances are surely lost in translation from the original Hebrew, it is still useful to understand the stories in the Tanakh or Hebrew Bible. The protagonist, Abraham (known first as Avram), is the founding patriarch of the Israelites. His story is contained in the section of Genesis known as *Lech-L'cha* (לֶךְ-לְךָ). This means "go to yourself," which is what is needed to start a spiritual journey. This story convenes God's covenant with the Hebrew people.

According to Jhos Singer, rabbi in residence at the Congregational Church of San Mateo, Genesis 12:1 should be looked at as a spiritual and mystical leaving. Where the text reads, "God said to Avram, go from your land/country..." a better translation would show God telling Avram, "Get out, go, get moving, go to yourself." The order of the leaving – from land, birthplace and father's house, is not logical or physical but rather

---

61 Gershon Winkler, The Way of the Boundary Crosser, An Introduction to Jewish Flexidoxy (Northvale, NJ: Jason Aronson, 1998), 21.

spiritual and mystical. Rabbi Singer believes shedding familial roots and taking up the spiritual path is a lifetime's work. "The Torah seems to understand that there is a big old personality and a kind of community personality and then a very, very intimate personality, all of which need to be shed in order to *Lech-L'cha* – to go to yourself."[62] Shedding these exterior trappings will aid in creating a clarity of purpose and vision, the First Pillar in the Seven Pillar methodology.

ETHICAL GUIDELINES, SOCIETAL ISSUES

The Torah can be viewed on many levels. It provides rules around which society can function. Consider the Ten Commandments: There are no other gods but God, no graven images; do not take God's name in vain – neither curse at God's name nor do things in the name of God that are not of God – observe the Sabbath, honor your parents, do not commit murder, engage in adultery, steal, lie about your neighbor or lust after your neighbor's house or spouse or servant or maid or ox or donkey.

The Torah also grapples with the important issues of social justice, including inequality and slavery. At the time it was written, an important distinction emerged between Israelite slavery and chattel slavery, in terms of bondage without free will. Both parties might expect to reap some benefit from the indentured servitude that characterized Israelite slavery: the indentured party would gain a certain measure of protection by joining a household, and the household would gain the labor. Torah mandated fairness to such slaves, including observing the Sabbath and feeding those in service as one would feed his own. Such consideration was held in stark contrast to forced, chattel slavery.

---

62 Jhos Singer, "Divine Paradox: Judaism 101" San Mateo, CA: Congregational Church of San Mateo, August 29, 2009.

FREEDOM FROM BONDAGE

The most important celebration of the Jewish year is Passover, which celebrates the story of Moses having led the Israelites out of bondage, after God wrought havoc on the Egyptians, passing over the Jewish households.[63] The eating of matzo at Passover is in memory of having to flee with no time for leavening the bread. Matzo is the bread of their flight, bread made with flour and water, without yeast. And the traditional cleansing of the house of all that is Hametz, or leavened, during Passover could be approached as a reminder that our things should not own or control us, and we should not be in bondage to property. [64] Likewise, it's good to take inventory of –and dispose of—that which is "fluff" or perhaps rises falsely within us.

It is easy to see how an idea inspired by the Torah's tale of slavery in Egypt could ignite compassion for others who are not free. Hence, the rituals of Passover are steeped in tradition, which can help free us today.

VALUING THE WORKER

Worker rights are strongly supported in the Torah. Consider the mandate of rest on the Seventh day, to celebrate being brought to freedom from slavery by the same God who also rested on the Seventh day. This mandate extends to everyone, including children, animals, and foreigners in your employ.[65] Employers are called to pay their workers on time: "If you hire poor people to work for you, don't hold back their pay, whether they are Israelites or foreigners who live in your town. Pay them their wages at the end of each

---

63 Exodus 5 (Shemot)

64 Gershon Winkler, *The Way of the Boundary Crosser, An Introduction to Jewish Flexidoxy,* (Northvale, NJ: Jason Aronson, 1998), 145.

65 Exodus 20 (Yitro) and Deuteronomy 5 (Va-'Ethannan)

day because they live in poverty and need the money to survive."[66] Social justice work in this area could involve advocating for a living wage: when employers do not give adequate wages, workers need to work more than one job just to make ends meet, and are thus prevented from observing a day of rest.

TZEDAKAH – CHARITY

The Hebrew word Tzedakah is based on tzedek (צֶדֶק), meaning righteousness, and the Torah is filled with prophetic calls to social justice and charity. Many of the Psalms – 33, 89, and 99 – speak of God's love of justice and righteousness, and many of the Proverbs do as well:

- **Proverb 13** [9] The light of the righteous is radiant; The lamp of the wicked is extinguished... brightly, but the lamp of the wicked is snuffed out...

- **Proverb 15** [6] In the house of the righteous there is much treasure, but in the harvest of the wicked there is trouble.

- **Proverb 16** [8] Better a little with righteousness than a large income with injustice...[11] Honest scales and balances are the Lord's; all the weights in the bag are His work...

- **Proverb 17** [13] Evil will never depart from the house of one who repays good with evil...[15] To acquit the guilty and convict the innocent—both are an abomination to the Lord ... [23] The wicked man draws a bribe out of his bosom to pervert the course of justice.

The Torah also contains in its pages the radical concept of isonomia or equality of souls, which indicates pure justice under God and before the law. Perhaps the most salient advice to the reader is found in Micah, 6.8: "He has told you, O man, what is good. And what the Lord requires of you: Only to do justice and

---

to love goodness, and to walk modestly with your God; then will your name achieve wisdom." This is echoed in Zechariah 7.9, and warnings against iniquity are found in Amos 5.11, Deuteronomy 10.17-19, and indeed throughout. The reason is clear: "For I, the Lord, love justice; I hate robbery with a burnt offering." (Isaiah 61.8)

MAIMONEDES' WISDOM

The Torah teachings specifically about charity were promoted beyond a Jewish following by *Moshe ben Maimon* (1137-1204), also known as Moses Maimonedes, one of the greatest Torah scholars of the Middle Ages. Maimonedes was court physician to Grand Vezier Alfadil, then to Sultan Saladin and his family. Invited to be Richard the Lionheart's personal physician, he declined, for even though Jews suffered under Islam, it was still safer as a Jew to live under an Islamic ruler than to enter Christian territory. In his writings, he outlined eight levels of giving, or Tzedakah (צדקה), to be considered part of the spiritual journey, from giving inadequately and hesitantly to giving the gift of independence.[67] The following graphic indicating the various levels to Tzedakah, broken down into stages along the journey and culminating in the highest, the gift of independence, helps explain the Tzedakah:

---

67 Erick Hoffman, *The Wisdom of Maimonides: The Life and Writings of the Jewish Sage* (Boston, MA: Trumpeter Press, 2008), 112.

ILLUSTRATION: THE LEVELS OF TZEDAKAH, OR CHARITY

GIFT OF INDEPENDENCE

Giving a person independence so they no longer need to depend on Tzedakah. There are four forms, greatest to the weakest:

1) Providing a poor person with work;
2) Making a partnership with that person—lower than work, as recipient might feel they're putting less into the partnership;
3) Giving an interest-free loan to a person in need;
4) Giving a grant to a person in need.

ANONYMOUS

Giving anonymously to a known recipient; giving anonymously to an unknown recipient via a wise and trustworthy person (or public fund) that can perform acts of Tzedakah using the funds in a most impeccable fashion.

NOT ANONYMOUS

Giving sadly; giving inadequately; giving adequately after being asked; Giving before being asked; giving publicly to an unknown recipient.

A Torah-observant social entrepreneur likely would find the Seven Pillar methodology quite useful in explaining and implementing these teachings about Tzedakah. For example, they might use the first pillar when discussing a vision that somehow fosters independence, so those receiving help may no longer depend on Tzedakah. Maimonides also spoke of collaborating with the recipient of Tzedakah. This, too, fits well with the Seven Pillar methodology through the Fourth Pillar, Partnership. It is exciting and gratifying to recognize how this relatively simple methodology is relevant across the broad spectrum of faith traditions.

A CHRISTIAN BASIS FOR SOCIAL ACTION

The Rev. Dr. James Keck, senior minister at First-Plymouth Congregational Church in Lincoln, Nebraska, has called social justice the very "heartbeat" of scripture, the Old Testament's code phrase for society's most vulnerable, the widow and the orphan, and culminating with Jesus.

> And then Jesus appears with his heartbeat. The spirit has anointed me to bring good news to the poor, to let the oppressed go free. I say to you love your neighbor as yourself. If someone asks you to give him your cloak, give him two. If he asks to walk a mile, walk two. How do you serve me, the Christ? When you feed the hungry, when you clothe the naked, when you visit those in prison.[68]

WHO WAS JESUS?

Not all who follow Jesus believe the same thing about him and there are many interpretations of his story. Yet there remains widespread agreement about some of the most basic facts. Jesus of Nazareth was born 2,000 years ago in what we now call the Middle East, during a brutal Roman occupation, and had an active ministry for about three years as a Jewish rabbi or teacher in about 30 CE.

The story of Jesus' life and death was chronicled in many Gospels (literally "good news"), four of which were selected for inclusion in the official canon, along with other documents

---

68   James Keck, May 30, 2010. "Holy, Holy, Holy in the Year That King Uzziah Died, Sermon #876" *Sermons of First-Plymouth Congregational Church, UCC*, (Lincoln, NE: First Plymouth Congregational Church, May 30, 2010), www.firstplymouth.org/sermons/10_sermons/05-30-10.pdf (accessed June 5, 2010).

including letters by early church leaders. These Gospels are Matthew, Mark and Luke, and John. The first three are known as the Synoptic Gospels because they share many of the same stories.

Luke is the Gospel to which we turn for the greatest number of parables about the poor. The Gospel of John is more spiritual and includes many miracles. It is the only Gospel in which Jesus speaks at any length about his own divinity. According to the Gospel of John, Jesus was God who pitched his tent among us for a time: the Logos (pattern) or Word of God made flesh, to teach us the Way, Truth and Life. To read this Gospel fully, it is important to understand certain subtleties. Truths are hidden in teachings written at a time when it would have been suicidal for a fledgling religion to criticize Rome, and when the new religion was struggling to differentiate itself from Judaism. Consider the mad man, overwhelmed by an evil legion, whom Jesus saves by casting the multitude into a herd of unclean swine (Mark 5).

Two of the Gospels trace Jesus' ancestry to Abraham. According to the genealogy in Matthew 1:1, fourteen generations arose between Abraham and David. From David to the Babylonian exile another 14 generations occurred, and from there to Jesus saw another 14 generations.[69]

This genealogy is different from those in the Old Testament because it includes women, some of whom were rather colorful. These are: Tamar, Rahab, Ruth, Uriah's wife (Bathsheba) and Mary. Tamar (Genesis 38:12-23) posed as a prostitute to seduce her father-in-law. Rahab (Joshua 2:6) was a prostitute from Jericho, who recognized the power of the Hebrew God and protected the scouts. Bathsheba was adulterous, faithful to the soldiers. Ruth (Ruth 3) was a Moabite foreigner. This unique genealogy can be good news to anyone who feels their own background somehow disqualifies

---

69 Howard, George. *Hebrew Gospel of Matthew.* (Macon, GA: Mercer University Press, 1995), 5.

them from good works.

Jesus, the Gospels relate, was a refugee from a murderous tyrant when he was a youth (Matthew 2:13), and he preached a social justice message that was both radically inclusive to all outcast groups – even women – and radically nonviolent. Even at the height of his popularity, even when people were shouting "Hosanna in the highest," Jesus chose to ride in to town on a humble colt, the foal of a donkey (Matthew 21:1-11). The Jewish people had been expecting a savior of the heroic sort, a Messiah to lead them out of bondage, entering the scene slaying a giant as David had with Goliath. Jesus was not what they expected. Instead, his message was one of peace and active non-violence.

Jesus was brutally executed under Pontius Pilate in the torturous manner that imperial Rome had perfected for those it chose to silence: the cross. Said Gershon Winkler, a scholar in Jewish law, history, theology and mysticism:

> Many of the greatest masters of Judaism were
> killed for empowering the people with their
> spiritual teachings, which the paranoid Roman
> Empire feared would lead to rebellion.[70]

Father John Dear, a Jesuit peace activist and former director of the Fellowship of Reconciliation, agrees, writing about the Roman soldiers who used to proclaim the "good news" Gospel of Caesar, and how anyone opposing Rome faced Jesus' fate.

> Because people lived in fear of being killed,
> everyone acceded to the empire's order. They
> did not know any alternative—nor could they
> imagine one. They were trapped under the vicious
> empire with no way out. Coming into this political

---

70 Winkler, 224, 227.

climate, Jesus' proclamation of "the good news of God's reign" is stunning in its daring challenge to Caesar, its bold vision of another way of life, and its radical hope in a loving, nonviolent God.[71]

It was in this context that Jesus spoke and acted out against injustice and corruption, with the inevitable and predictable consequences: he was crucified. After quoting Psalm 22, His last radical act of loving non-violence was to forgive those who had put him to death. According to the Gospel of John, in Verse 18, Pilate, in interrogating Jesus, said, "So you are a king!" Jesus answered, "You are the one saying that I am a king. This is why I came into the world, to bear witness to the truth. And everyone who belongs to the truth listens to me." To Jesus, portrayed in the Gospel as the *embodiment* of Truth, Pilate asked, blindly, "What is truth?"

Many have staked their lives on the belief that Jesus was the Way, the Truth and the Life, and the foretold Messiah, arguing that he fulfilled 48 or more ancient messianic prophecies.[72] Others who reject Jesus argue that because Jesus did not bring about an end to his people's suffering through an imposed peace, and because his banner has been used to justify numerous travesties, he was in fact a dangerous misleader. For those interested in exploring this topic further, a good analysis is available in Roy Williams' text *God, Actually*.[73] Whatever your view about Jesus' divinity, there is evidence for his historical existence, within and outside the Gospels, and for following the wisdom he left behind.

---

71 John Dear, Transfiguration; A Meditation on Transforming Ourselves and Our World, (New York, NY: Doubleday, 2007) 24.

72 Lee Strobel, *The Case for Christ: A Journalist's Personal Investigation of the Evidence for Jesus*, DVD, directed by Michael Eaton and Timothy Eaton (Los Angeles, CA: Lions Gate. 2007).

73 Roy Williams. God, Actually: Why God Probably Exists, Why Jesus Was Probably Divine, and Why the "Rational" Objections to Religion are Unconvincing. (Oxford: Lion. 2009).

WHAT DID JESUS TEACH?

Jesus' Good News interpretation of the law likely resulted in domestic discord (Matthew 10:34). First, he proclaimed a year of Jubilee, or yovel, the year at the end of seven cycles of sabbatical years. Not only were God's people commanded to keep a Sabbath day holy; they were to observe the *shemittah*, another holy period of rest, every seven years: letting the land lie fallow for a year so as not to deplete its nutrients, and forgiving their debts as a way of redistributing the wealth (Leviticus 25:4; Deuteronomy 15:1-2). And every forty nine years (seven times every seven years), in a yovel cycle, the land was to return to the original owners who had lived on it before being forced off due to financial difficulties.[74]

In Luke's Gospel, when Jesus went into the temple to read Isaiah, he referred directly to this tradition, which had fallen into disuse: "The Spirit of the Lord is on me because he has anointed me to proclaim good news to the poor. He has sent me to proclaim freedom for the prisoners and recovery of sight for the blind, to set the oppressed free, to proclaim the year of the Lord's favor." Then he rolled up the scroll and told them, "Today this scripture is fulfilled in your hearing" (Luke 4:16-21). Not only had he implied his position, he had challenged the power elite to reinstate Jubilee, something he surely knew would bring him disfavor and danger.

Jesus was all the more radical in proffering a message that no person should be objectified, regardless of gender; all are of value in God's eyes. He accepted all comers, proclaiming both the forgiveness of sin and the healing of the body, with an apparently supernatural disregard for the mores and taboos of society, as he ministered to the men and women around him. In the sense that the word *charismatic* arises from the word *joy*, Jesus was a charismatic leader, but he was humble. When someone called him "good

---

74 Winkler, 156.

teacher," he replied, "Why do you call me good? No one is good –
except God alone." (Mark 10:18).

For Jesus' social justice message, there's no better place to
start than with Luke. Seventeen of Jesus' most cutting parables
that touch on social justice, power, mercy and social station can be
found in the Gospel of Luke.

SOCIAL JUSTICE PARABLES IN THE GOSPEL OF LUKE

Barren Fig Tree [13:6-8]	Dishonest Manager [16:1-13]	Door Closes [13:24-30]
Faithful Servants [12:35-48]	Good Father (Prodigal Son) [15:11-32]	Good Samaritan [10:25-37]
Help at Midnight [11:5-10]	How to Be a Guest [14:7-14]	King & Tower-Builder [14:28-32]
Lazarus/ Rich Man [16:19-31]	Lost Coin [15:8-10]	Pharisee & Tax Collector [18:9-14]
Rich Fool [12:16-21]	Servant's Reward [17:7-10]	Ten Minas [19:11-27]
Two Debtors [7:41-43]	Unjust Judge [18:1-8]	

Jesus spoke in the language of his time, using vivid imagery
of his day – some of which, (raw salt, flocks of sheep, and fig
trees) readers of today may find unfamiliar or strange. But he also
commented on urban realities in the increasingly urban landscape
of his time. For example, in Luke 13, Jesus discusses the Tower of
Siloam falling and killing 18 people, in order to make a theological
point that tragedies happen to good and bad alike—and that there is
a need for everyone to change his or her ways.

Perhaps the best known of the parables is about Lazarus and
the Rich Man (Luke 16:19-31). Lazarus, alone at the unnamed rich
man's gate, is so weak he cannot even stop the dogs from licking his

sores. He is entirely alone in his poverty, and he receives not even a crumb from the rich man. Later, when the theater of life is over and the masks of social station are removed and each is judged, the rich man finds himself in hell and asks for Lazarus to be sent with just a drop of water on his finger to quench his thirst. But it is impossible because there is a chasm between them that Lazarus, in Heaven, cannot cross over.

St. John Chrysostom (of the golden mouth), an important early church father who lived and preached in Antioch at about AD 350, gave seven sermons on the parable of Lazarus and the Rich Man, which can be read in his book *On Wealth and Poverty*. Chrysostom was born to family that was well off and highly educated. He renounced his roots to live in austerity as a monk before returning to the greater worlds to serve as a priest. He most knew what he was preaching about. Chrysostom used the parable to address many of the enduring issues of poverty, noting that we cannot judge poverty or ill health as a punishment for a sin, because we cannot know why some people suffer and some live in abundance.

In contrast to the biblical message that the poor are suffering while we feast and that we must do something about that, our popular mythology allows us to turn away from the suffering of others and enjoy our own prosperity. All this runs counter to what Jesus taught. In the Gospel of Matthew, the Bible says: "For I was hungry and you gave me something to eat, I was thirsty and you gave me something to drink, I was a stranger and you invited me in." (Matthew 25:35, NIV).

Dr. Richard Saller, Dean of the School of Humanities and Sciences at Stanford University, reminds us that Jesus' statement of "you have the poor always with you" was realistic, given the limited potential of the Roman Empire, and notes that,

In a near-subsistence economy, the average standard

of living for individuals was roughly one tenth of
what Americans on average enjoy today. The only
way the philosopher Seneca, writing in the first
century A.D., could imagine a society of equality was
to assume that every Roman would be poor.[75]

When Jesus told his followers that "the poor will always be
with you," he was quoting Deuteronomy 15:11, and his listeners
would know that the next line commands us to open our hands to
the poor. He also gave us a roadmap for how to put our work into
practice. As Dean Saller pointed out, later in his speech,

Today the fact that poverty is still with us in
a society that's ten times as rich can only be
described as a tragedy. But rather than just
lamenting the tragedy, we need to understand why
it is so, so that we can do something about it.

To say that Jesus' teachings are of serious interest to both
Jimmy and Rosalynn Carter would be to understate the case.
President Carter had an evangelical upbringing and is a practicing
Christian – even with his busy schedule, he manages to teach
Sunday school 30 times a year. So it seems logical that any advice
that he might give would be grounded in his faith and would
therefore have biblical roots.

As I studied President Carter's advice to me, I was struck by
how well it worked as a practical way to implement the Beatitudes.
I became so convinced of a relationship between the Beatitudes
and the Seven Pillars that I wrote a doctoral dissertation about it in
2011. In the next set of essays, each Beatitude and its relationship
with the Seven Pillars is examined.

---

75 Richard Saller, *A Concert for Hope*, a documentary short by Lauren Speeth
(Burlingame, CA: Elfenworks Productions, 2011), online at www.inequality.com.

THE SPIRITUAL NATURE OF SEVEN

The choice of exactly seven Pillars was a natural, spiritual decision; the number seven is associated with wholeness and completeness, and although it is not always positive – Satan has seven heads in Revelation 12:3 – in biblical numerology, it is generally considered the number of spiritual perfection.

SPIRITUAL, NOT DOCTRINE

Throughout the centuries, much persecution of the innocent has taken place in the name of doctrine, whether specifically religious or state-sanctioned and rationalist. In these essays, I illustrate some of the similar philosophies among some of the great religions with which I am familiar, and the Seven Pillar methodology, placing a particular emphasis on the Beatitudes. Without being doctrinaire, your faith can inform your work.

It is my hope that practitioners of many wisdom and faith traditions can apply the Seven Pillars and find concordance. While the Pillars can be viewed as grounded in the Beatitudes (Matthew 5:3-10), detailed in the following pages, are universal truths that can be found in other faith traditions and other paths, as well.

ESSAY QUESTIONS

1. *Discuss the principle for charity common to Judaism, Islam, Christianity and Buddhism.*

2. *Consider: What is my tradition and how does it inform the way I view the world and my work?*

3. *Consider: What do I feel about Jesus' teachings, including the Beatitudes? Does the controversial nature of Jesus tend to preclude them from my work? Why or why not?*

ESSAY SET 2: BEATITUDES

In the Gospel of Matthew, Jesus' official teaching is presented at the Sermon on the Mount. Addressing the crowd, Jesus presents eight poetic, creative, and beautiful Beatitudes as a blessing to the assembled crowd. And it's not an impossibility to apply the Beatitudes to daily life. Jesus' eight Beatitudes can be said to summarize Jesus' teaching. Below is my own translation:

TRANSLATION OF THE BEATITUDES

- Blessed are the poor in spirit, for theirs are the heavens.
- Blessed are those who mourn, for they shall be comforted.
- Blessed are those whose strength is under control, for they shall inherit the earth.
- Blessed are those hungering and thirsting for what's right and just; for they shall be satisfied.
- Blessed are the merciful, for they shall obtain mercy.
- Blessed are the innocent-hearted, for they shall see God.
- Blessed are the peacemakers, for they shall be called children of God.
- Blessed are those persecuted for the cause of justice, for theirs is heaven's kingdom.

--The Beatitudes of Matthew, Matthew 5:3-10

Each Beatitude sets the groundwork for the next, and although they have been described in many ways, to me it makes sense to look at them as necessary layers in a geological formation, leading to solid rock from which to build. This metaphor works in another way: the Beatitudes are a useful set of guiding principles on which to base a life. In that way, they're similar to the Seven Pillars. To my mind, they are a useful foundation on which to base a Seven Pillar framework:

ILLUSTRATION: THE BEATITUDES AS BEDROCK

Throughout the Beatitudes, one constant remains present: a humble attitudinal foundation, as summarized by this simple teaching in Matthew 22:37-39, where Jesus, quoting Deuteronomy 6:5 and Leviticus 19:18, states: "Love the Lord your God with all your heart, soul, and mind." This is the first and most important commandment. The second most important commandment is similar; "Love others as much as you love yourself." Through following his Beatitudes, Jesus promises a state of blessedness in the here and now.

THE BEATITUDES: A LANGUAGE LESSON

It may come as a surprise to find that scholarly debate is ongoing about the language in which this gospel was written, whether Greek, Hebrew or even Aramaic. Fascinated by this controversy, I looked into all three languages to help shed light on the Beatitudes. During my research, my *Interlinear Bible: Hebrew-Greek-English* text was insufficient because, despite the book's title, the Gospel of Matthew was only presented in Greek and English. Someday, it would be helpful to have an interlinear Bible that also presents Matthew in Hebrew. Meanwhile, I have sought other sources. Rather than take sides, I presented the Beatitudes in Aramaic, Hebrew, Greek and English, and have included nekudot (the vowel dots and lines that help with pronunciation) as a pronunciation guide as well as concordance numbers. You will find it in Appendix A.

I lean to the view that the Gospel of Matthew originally might have been written in Hebrew, whereas other gospels, such as the Gospel of Luke, likely were not. Here's why. As Daniel J. Harrington, Chair of the Biblical Studies Department at Boston College School of Theology and Ministry points out, "The Beatitudes are thoroughly Jewish in form and content."[76] Jesus, who was a rabbi, would have been teaching from a Hebrew Torah, and Matthew is sometimes referred to as the "Gospel for the Jewish People."

What's more, the Greek version of Matthew, which may be a translation from Hebrew, isn't as articulate as the Greek in the other Gospels; it does not trip off the tongue. Luke's Greek is beautiful and easy for a Greek scholar to read, whereas Matthew's Gospel is not lovely in Greek. But in Hebrew, Matthew's Gospel has a beautiful flow and cadence, with Hebraisms, nuances, puns and alliterations. It also has the sort of lyrical parallelism often seen in ancient Hebrew biblical poetry[77] where the second line adds to the first (synthetic parallelism), and the last distich (couplet) echoes the first. In Hebrew, Matthew's Gospel also uses word plays that bring the beginning and endings of chapters together in ways that are not present in the Greek version.[78] Additionally, some copies of

---

76 Harrington, 84.

77 George Buchanan Gray, *The Forms of Hebrew Poetry Considered with Special Reference to the Criticism and Interpretation of the Old Testament* (London: Hodder & Stoughton, 1915), 237.

78 George Howard, *Hebrew Gospel of Matthew* (Macon, GA: Mercer University Press, 1995), 184-190.

the ancient Syriac (Aramaic) versions of the Gospel, standard for the Eastern Orthodox Church, mention it was taken from Hebrew.

Another researcher into Matthew's roots, author James Scott Trimm, quotes the Petishah Aramaic Matthew manuscript as ending with the following quote: "Completion of the Holy Gospel as published by Matthew; and which he published in Hebrew, in the land of the Palestinians."[79] Another ancient Hebrew Matthew text, the *B'sorot Matti*, has been said by some scholars, including Trimm, to include evidence of pre-Greek origins. Trimm cites as evidence for the Hebrew source, the listing of the full 14 names in Jesus' lineage (as expected in Matthew 1:17), various Hebraisms, and the presence of the HaShem (three dots) to indicate the name of God. If it were a translation from the Greek word for *Lord, Kurios*, it would yield Adonai, not HaShem.[80] Finally, a later source for Hebrew is the 14th century Hebrew polemic treatise, *The Touchstone*, by Shem-Tob ben-Isaac ben-Shaprut.

Nehemia Gordon, a Karaite Jew and founder of the World Karaite Movement, notes that as early as the First century CE, Bishop Papias of Hierapolis wrote that Matthew μεν συν εβραιδι διαλεκώ τα λόγια συνεταξατο ηρύηνευσεν δ αυτα ώς ήν δυνατος εκαοτος ("Matthew collected the oracles [literally: "words"] in the Hebrew language and each interpreted them as best he could."[81])

Trimm makes a compelling case for the Hebrew origins of Matthew, quoting many early church fathers and outside sources, including Epiphanius, Jerome, Papias, and Isho'Dad.[82] From Iraneus' *Against Heresies*, Chapter 3:1: "Matthew also issued

---

79 James Scott Trimm, *B'Sorot Matti: The Good News According to Matthew from An Old Hebrew Manuscript* (Hurst, TX: Hebrew/Aramaic New Testament Research Institute, 1990), xii.

80 Ibid., viii.

81 Nehemia Gordon, *The Hebrew Yeshua* vs. the Greek Jesus (Arlington, TX: Hilkiah Press, 2005), 76.

82 Trimm, x-xii.

a written Gospel among the Hebrews in their own dialect."[83] Trimm quotes Eusebius, who is, in turn, quoting Origen, "The first [Gospel] is written according to Matthew, the same that was once a tax collector, but afterwards an emissary of Yeshua the Messiah, who having published it for the Jewish believers, wrote it in the Hebrew."[84] These and other authors also point out the Hebrew word "play" used in the text, which is not found in the Greek. Trimm writes, perhaps controversially:

> If the Protestant movement had broken off from the Eastern rather than Western Church, Protestantism would be, on the whole, arguing in favor of Aramaic rather than Greek. We have [more than] 350 ancient manuscripts of the Petishah (dating to around the 5th century) and George Lamsa has a good argument that the Petishah Aramaic predates the Greek text (or perhaps I might alternatively offer, is based on a Hebrew or Aramaic text that predates the Greek).

This statement may seem extreme, but there exists enough controversy about the Gospel of Matthew to make it worthwhile to study every possible language.

BLESSEDNESS

The first two words of each Beatitude are of such special significance; they are repeated every time: *Blessed are.* Jesus is speaking of the blessedness of people in the here and now. He does not say *blessed will be.* The words are *blessed are,* in the present tense. In contrast with the gospel of sin, wretchedness, guilt and

---

83 Ibid., xi.
84 Ibid., xi.

shame, which is so often preached, this is Jesus' lesson about a state of blessedness now. His Beatitudes are a recipe for happiness, a present and joyful state.

The Hebrew word for *blessed* is *ashrei* (אשרי) and the Greek is μακαριο, *makarios*. The Hebrew *ashrei* is probably more precisely translated as *happy*, and it usually indicates satisfaction or contentment. This is a significant point not always acknowledged in discussions of the Beatitudes. The Russian translation from the Greek μακαριο holds nuances that can inform our English interpretation.

The word Блаженый (*Blazhenny*) means more than just *happy* (those who)." The word Blag (Blazhen, Блажен) is related to God's nature, and God's nature is good. So, Блаженый means that "you have God's nature within."[85] According to the Russian interpretation, Jesus' Beatitudes are teaching a path to God nature. This relates well to the Aramaic of Jesus' day, where there is no verb, and the Beatitudes likely would have read, simply, "O Blessedness." As Scottish theologian William Barclay points out, the Beatitude "is the statement of joyous thrill and the radiant gladness of the Christian life. In the face of the Beatitudes, a gloom-encompassed Christianity is unthinkable."[86]

Each Beatitude sets the groundwork for the next, as St. John Chrysostom pointed out in his writings long ago.[87] They proceed from an internal to an outward focus. The first three Beatitudes have been called the contemplative virtues. They are followed by the active virtues. The Beatitudes have been alternatively described as: a ladder, golden chain, solid bedrock, an interrelated circle,

---

85 Alex Valiuski, email consultation with Lauren Speeth, April 17, 2010.

86 William Barclay, *The Gospel of Matthew, Volume One, The New Daily Study Bible Series*, rev. ed., (Philadelphia, PA: Westminster Press, 1975), 88.

87 A Monk of St. Tikhon's Monastery, ed. *These Truths We Hold - The Holy Orthodox Church: Her Life and Teachings* (South Canaan, PA: St. Tikhon's Seminary Press) 1986.

or facets of a diamond.[88] All of these metaphors work because the Beatitudes are a useful set of guiding principles on which to establish one's higher self.

The Beatitudes are a set of contrasts in which a positive is paired with a negative: sad against happy, thirst against satisfaction. Jesus' Beatitudes are beautiful to read; pure, plaintive poetry. From this perspective it is interesting to note that in Greek, the first four Beatitudes start with the letter π (*pi*): the poor (πτωχοι – *ptochoi*), those who mourn (πενθουντες – *penthountes*), the meek (πραεις – *praus*), and those who hunger for righteousness (πεινωντες – *peinontes*).

ILLUSTRATION: PILLARS AND BEATITUDES

FIRST BEATITUDE – POOR...IN SPIRIT

The first Beatitude is an attitudinal foundation on which other Beatitudes are built. Translations vary and include the simple "happy are the poor" and "happy are those who take sides with the

88 Jim Forest, St. John Chrysostom, Rev. Matthew Riddle, and Bill and Michael Dodds.

poor," meaning that God does – and we should also – comfort those who are poor. It is false pride to consider oneself an island. Without others and without God, we are all poor. Westmount College Biblical scholar Robert Gundry points out that the Hebrew words for poor (*aniyei* - עֲנִי) and meek (*anavim* - עֲנָיו) are largely synonymous, so the addition of "in spirit" helps clarify the English meaning.[89]

It is important not to gloss over the revolutionary nature of this first Beatitude. In a world based on appearances, where most everyone is expected to answer "fine" to the perfunctory question, "How are you?" Jesus offers us the relief of taking off the suffocating mask and admitting our own brokenness.

Or, we can continue, like Peter Pan, to run away from our own shadow, refusing to grow up and never developing the capacity for compassion. In Jesus' day, the pagan world despised pity. The ancient Egyptians[90] and the Pharisees related misfortunes and illness to sin,[91] and the Eastern world related it to karma.[92] Jesus offered grace.

The practitioner who uses the Beatitudes as bedrock has, at the basis of this first Beatitude, trust in a higher inspiration. The first Beatitude calls for an empty vessel, a social entrepreneur who is "poor in spirit" yet open to God's voice, trusting in His inspiration. According to the second and fourth Beatitudes, this may involve mourning the state of the world and continuing to hunger and thirst for righteousness.

Through contemplative wisdom arises discernment of what the true justice issues are, and a burning desire to pursue them. How

---

89 Gundry, 69.

90 Rosalie David, *Religion and Magic in Ancient Egypt* (New York, NY: Penguin Books, 2002), 278.

91 Hector Avalos, *Health Care and the Rise of Christianity* (Peabody, Mass: Hendrickson Books, 1999), 23-24.

92 Robert Ellwood and Barbara McGraw, *Many Peoples, Many Faiths: Women and Men in the World Religions, Ninth Edition* (Upper Saddle River, NJ: Prentice Hall, 2009), 53.

can we be sure our vision is authentically inspired? Jesuit peace activist Fr. John Dear offers simple counsel: Spend some time every single day, listening to God and cultivating silence and a quiet spirit. All we have to do is listen. With inner peace, within our own inner garden, we can begin to build peace in the world. This means making peace with our inner demons. This requires mindfulness and solitude – states of being Americans irrationally fear and find so unfamiliar. But it is in solitude that we find our gentleness, and it is there that the still, small voice of God can be known and heard. Dear writes, "As we dwell in solitude and cultivate interior silence, we learn to listen for the consoling whispers of God. In solitude or even in a crowded park or quiet gathering of people, silence can be a doorway to the peace of God."[93] Besides listening, we need to begin the work of letting go, both of clinging, and of our image of God. Our culture discourages this sort of letting go, this sort of radical faith and vulnerability that Jesus taught and that St. Francis followed. Of course Jesus and others who followed authentically often suffered greatly, but as Dear counsels, a life of peace will involve a journey of letting go.

Without the radical recognition of the poverty and brokenness of our human condition, we will never reach self-transformation and move beyond our boundless ego to even begin looking at the second Beatitude. Growing up and out of childishness doesn't mean disaster; Jesus promises comfort. It may seem obvious that one cannot add anything to a vessel that is already full, but the concept of being so full of the "right" answers that one cannot see new solutions is also contained in this Beatitude. So is the concept of "beginner's mind." When you realize you are empty, God can begin to fill you up; here lies the kingdom (βασιλεια – *basileia*) of heaven (ουρανων – *ouranos*). From this knowledge arises inspiration or vision, the first Pillar.

---

93 John Dear, *Living Peace: A Spirituality of Contemplation and Action* (New York, NY: Doubleday, 2004), 26.

SECOND BEATITUDE – THOSE WHO MOURN

The second Beatitude centers on the word for mourning, πενθουντες—*penthountes*[94] in Greek, *haAvelim* (הָאֲבֵלִים) in Hebrew—and then presents a promise of the very opposite. How can this be? Perhaps once we realize, with the first Beatitude, that we are in a state of poverty, we are likely to mourn. This is a very strong word. According to Barclay, *penthountes* is the "strongest word for mourning in the Greek language."[95] This is deep, sorrowful mourning. Is it for the state of the world or own failures? Jesus does not say. What Jesus is saying is that mourning is the correct next response to have (not anger or blame).

This second Beatitude is another matched pair of opposites. Happy are those who mourn or weep, for they will laugh or be comforted. Feel the mourning over the sorry state of the world, over the losses, whatever they may be. Perhaps if we regret but do not blame, and realize that things are the way things are, we can move forward toward shalom building.

Perhaps we can consider the original meaning of the word for Satan in Hebrew, *ha-Satan* (הַשָּׂטָן) which means "the accuser," before indulging in schadenfreude or throwing blame and accusations around. Jesus also was known as the consoler, or *Menahhem*, and this teaching harkens to Isaiah 11.

Those who mourn are blessed; they shall know the healing balm of God's comfort. In the *Shem Tov Hebrew Matthew*, the translator chooses the word "wait" and not "mourn" – those who wait for the Lord will be comforted. This is not necessarily a contradiction if you mourn and, in a state of openness, wait for the Lord's comfort.

---

94 Strong's Concordance, Greek, "3996," http://strongsnumbers.com/greek/3996. htm (accessed May 2, 2010).

95 Barclay, 93.

THIRD BEATITUDE – THE MEEK

The third Beatitude promises that the meek shall inherit the earth, which tends to sound like a contradiction. This is true only until the word "meek" is examined more closely. The English word derives from the Greek πραεις (*praus*), or strength under control. Strong's Greek Dictionary entry 4239, πραΰς, notes that *praus* (prah-ooce'), or meek, is apparently a primary word, mild and, by implication, humble and meek.[96] Author Raniero Cantalamessa points out that the French word is *doux* (soft), the word Luther used *Sanftmütigen* (meek or sweet), and the word used in an ecumenical German Bible means nonviolent.[97]

Ethics and business professor David Gill of Gordon-Conwell Theological Seminary relates this concept of meek to being "gentle and tame, to let go... giving up control and resting in freedom."[98] The path to meekness, according to Gill, is to "Let go, be still; wait and hope in the Lord."

Leading Greek Scholar Dr. William Barclay notes that Aristotle defined *praotes* as a happy midpoint, halfway between excessive anger (*orgilotes*) and excessive angerlessness (*aorgesia*),[99] and so the word has been used to refer to a colt that has been broken for riding, a soothing medicine, and a sailor's gentle breeze.[100] Author Michael Crosby, a Capuchin Franciscan, notes that "a heart that is *a-praus* will not only be in a dynamic of violence, but this violence will be grounded in the need to control some aspect of our power,

---

96 Strong's Concordance, Greek, "4239," http://strongsnumbers.com/greek/4239. htm (accessed May 2, 2010).

97 Raniero Cantalamessa; translated by Marsha Daigle-Williamson, *Beatitudes: Eight Steps to Happiness*. (Cincinnati: Servant Books, 2009), 33.

98 David Gill, *Becoming Good: Building Moral Character* (Downers Grove, IL: IVP Books, 2000), 139.

99 Barclay, 90.

100 David Gill, in a meeting with the author, Burlingame, CA, January 22, 2010.

possessions, and prestige."[101]

To Michael H. Crosby, author of *Spirituality of the Beatitudes: Matthew's Vision for the Church in an Unjust World*, the spiritual journey moves from a child level, where societal belonging is defined by adhering to the Ten Commandments, through the adolescent level, where group belonging includes religion's rituals, to a spiritual level, the "Domain of Spirituality." It is this third level to which the Beatitudes belong.[102] Moses, in Numbers 12:3, is cited as meek, and Jesus is also referred to as meek in Matthew 11:29. In this definition, meek applies to one who has one's strength under control, and knows when to submit to God and how to keep one's anger in check. This can be very effective. This is the sort of leader in whose hands the world will be safe, so it is well that this Beatitude has been translated as "Splendid are those who are gentle; the world will be safe in their hands."[103]

The first three Beatitudes run contrary to the childish nature of an undisciplined ego. If a person does not have the ego under control, she or he is not likely to be effective for the long term. We now transition to the active Beatitudes. They bring to mind the phrase "march on," the translation offered by John Dear, SJ, in the film *A Narrow Path*.

Social entrepreneurs who do not have their perspective clear or who do not have a pure heart or who aren't peacemakers in their work could covet personal accolades rather than authentically sharing the credit for any accomplishments. Without understanding the virtues spelled out in the first three Beatitudes, they might resent giving away the credit, seek ways at ego gratification or simply burn out.

---

101 Michael H. Crosby, *Spirituality of the Beatitudes: Matthew's Vision for the Church in an Unjust World* (Maryknoll, NY: Orbis Books, 2005), 93.

102 Ibid., xiv.

103 John Henson, *Good as New, A Radical Retelling of the Scriptures* (Alresford, UK: John Hunt Publishing, 2004), 129.

FOURTH BEATITUDE – THOSE HUNGERING FOR RIGHTEOUSNESS

This Beatitude promises soul satisfaction to those whose appetite for justice is insatiable. In this Beatitude, Jesus is taking a cue from the "weeping prophet" of the Torah, Jeremiah, who "makes it clear that the promise of finding a relationship with God is conditional, and the promise of experiencing liberation is conditional. The condition: pursuing justice and peace, even in the midst of captivity."[104] It is as if Jesus were saying, "March on, you who are hungering and thirsting after righteousness (δικαιοσυνην - *dikaiosuné*, righteousness, equity, justification or *dikaios*),[105] that is where you will find joy." This hungering and thirsting is sometimes translated as personal rightness, sometimes as justice in a societal and holistic sense. English gives us no way to convey both meanings.

When working for change, a continuous discontent will help keep you motivated, especially when the discontent is not only with the world, but with your own effectiveness. Why not cultivate a mindset that is ever searching for better results? I know that while I am sometimes overjoyed at the impact of The Elfenworks Foundation, which was established to create change in new and different ways, I am never contented. And I know this mindset helps me keep our focus.

For Jesus, who was once a refugee, justice does not affect the citizen alone. Jesus adds the "stranger" to the list of those for whom justice must be sought: "For I was hungry and you gave me something to eat, I was thirsty and you gave me something to drink, I was a stranger and you invited me in," (Matthew 25:35-36 NIV).

---

104 Brian McLaren, Elisa Padilla, and Ashley Bunting Seeber, *The Justice Project* (Grand Rapids, MI: Baker Books 2009), 83.

105 Strong's Concordance, Greek, "1343," http://strongsnumbers.com/greek/1343. htm (accessed May 2, 2010).

Jesus does not promise that we will find justice in this imperfect world.

We can summarize the first four Beatitudes of Jesus' teachings by saying those who are always vigilant and constantly aware that the world needs help, and are resolved to make a positive difference, can be trusted to get good things done, find joy and be fully satisfied.

These first four Beatitudes all complement the Seven Pillars. A person with "poverty of spirit" will not be open to inspiration without a change of heart. One who mourns the state of the world, who is meek, and who continually hungers for justice will be motivated to employ skills (#2) in a non-duplicative (#3) partnership with others (#4), share the credit (#5), accept feedback (#6), and be filled up again by God, along the bumpy path (#7). The meek, who clarify their purpose, their value and their sense of self, are more likely to be the sort of partners, bosses, co-workers we would wish to have "inherit the earth."

ILLUSTRATION: RELATING BEATITUDES TO SEVEN PILLARS

Vision	Special Skills	Non-Duplication	Partnership	Credit Sharing	Feedback	Staying Power	BEATITUDES
●	●	●	●	●	●	●	1. Oh Blessedness of the poor in spirit, for theirs is the kingdom of heaven.
●	●	●	●	●	●	●	2. Oh Blessedness of those who mourn, for they shall be comforted.
●	●	●	●	●	●	●	3. Oh Blessedness of the meek, for they shall inherit the earth.
●	●	●	●	●	●	●	4. Oh Blessedness of they who hunger and thirst for righteousness; they shall be satisfied.
●	●	●	●	●	●	●	5. Oh Blessedness of the merciful, for they shall obtain mercy.
●	●	●	●	●	●	●	6. Oh Blessedness of the pure of heart, for they shall see God.
●	●	●	●	●	●	●	7. Oh Blessedness of the peacemakers, for they shall be called children of God.
●	●	●	●	●	●	●	8. Oh Blessedness of they who are persecuted for the sake of righteousness; theirs is the kingdom of heaven.

FIFTH BEATITUDE – THE MERCIFUL

In an imperfect world, where one cannot expect to find perfect justice, mercy and forgiveness are the basis of peacemaking. If we have taken to heart the earlier Beatitudes and have recognized the shadows that eclipse our perspectives and the failings that block our progress, we realize we have been forgiven much, and should be likewise generous. So march on, you who are merciful, for you will find mercy. The Hebrew word for mercy, *chesed* (חֶסֶד) spelled with a ח chet ס samech and ד dalet, does not have an English counterpart. It refers not only to assistance but to the sincere empathy for the person to whom you will offer compassion. This has been translated as "loving kindness" or "steadfast love," and it is the basis of Hasidic Judaism.

Likewise, the Greek word for mercy, *eleémón* (ελεημονες[106] - merciful), the root for which is *eleos*, is multifaceted and replete with meaning. Not only can it include an attitude of forgiveness, it also can involve active intervention and healing. Jesus' ministry is typified by mercy, and the word is used elsewhere to show his actions, including associating with and actively forgiving others. Later in the Gospel of Matthew, Jesus points his followers to the Torah teachings in Hosea 6:6, saying, "But go and learn what this means: 'I desire mercy, not sacrifice.' For I have not come to call the righteous, but sinners." (Matthew 9:12-13, NIV).

We all can find moments in which to show mercy, with the right mindset. Author Tod Lindberg, a Research Fellow at Stanford University, says, "Mercy is a quality within reach of everyone at one time or another. All mercy requires is a position of the barest advantage over another, even for the most fleeting of moments."[107]

---

106 Strong's Concordance, Greek, "1655," http://strongsnumbers.com/greek/1655.htm (accessed May 2, 2010).

107 Tod Lindberg, "What the Beatitudes Teach." *Policy Review*, September 2007, 9-10.

This Beatitude uses the same word, mercy, in both action and reaction: The merciful will find mercy (ελεημονες / ελεηθησονται). Catholics list seven spiritual and seven corporal works of mercy. The corporal works are feed, give drink to, clothe and shelter those in need, comfort those in prison, visit the sick, and bury the dead. The spiritual works are admonish sin, instruct the ignorant, comfort the sorrowful, counsel the doubtful, be patient with those in error, forgive offenses, and pray for all – living and dead.[108]

Your vision as a social entrepreneur requires mercy. It offers mercy to the earth, or to some constituency about which you care very deeply. Otherwise, you wouldn't be reading this book. Mercy is at the heart of vision, the First Pillar. Understanding how to develop empathy as a path to compassion is a Special Skill (Pillar Two), which sets you apart as a social entrepreneur and manager. Your ability to be merciful will enable you to better work in partnerships, to better obtain and apply feedback, and to better share the credit. It will help you stay the course, long term (Pillar Seven).

SIXTH BEATITUDE – THE PURE IN HEART

When we look to the context of others, purely with a good heart, and we act with good intentions, God is with us, and we are able to recognize God working in and through others. This could, perhaps, refer to being one's true inherent self, not being caught up in ego and the vanities of this world. This Beatitude also has been translated as "March on, you who are pure of heart; you will see God," and "Splendid are those who seek the best for others and not themselves: They will have God for company."[109]

---

108 Day, Dorothy. Selected Writings. Maryknoll, NY: Orbis Books, 2007, 98.
109 Henson, 129.

SEVENTH BEATITUDE – THE PEACEMAKERS

In Greek, this Beatitude centers on the word ειρηνοποιοι,[110] or peacemaker. In Hebrew, the word *Osei Shalom* (עוֹשֵׂי שָׁלוֹם) means makers of peace. Shalom involves reconciliation, a restoration of wholeness, which is a true peace. *Osei* is an active verb that involves doing or making. Peace is something we make.

This is not the imposed peace by the will of the empire; that was Pax Romana. Jesus led by example when, rather than flee the imminent trial, accused as a traitor to the empire, he peacefully accepted execution at the hands of Rome's imperial power. When one is able to do the real work of peace (to reconcile people, resolve differences, restore wholeness, and bring about true shalom) one is rightly behaving as a child of God.

The Greek word *υιοι* (sons) can refer to women as well as men, and the Hebrew word *B'nei* (בְּנֵי) also is valid in translation as "children," all children. Peacemaking is everyone's work. Although in older translations one often finds "sons of God," newer and friendlier translations are intentionally more inclusive, using the words "children of God" or "sons and daughters of God."

Jesuit peace activist John Dear writes, "God's grace of nonviolence liberates us from the personal, social and systemic sin of violence. In the light of nonviolence, God's grace heals us personally from our violence, roots us in the peace of Christ, transforms us into peacemakers and transforms our violent world into God's nonviolent reign of justice and peace."[111] Dear also offers insight into the difficulty of peacemaking: "Why do so few find the narrow gate, the narrow path to life? Because it is hard to be sane when the culture around us is insane. It is hard to speak of

---

110 Strong's Concordance, Greek, "1518," http://strongsnumbers.com/greek/1518. htm (accessed May 2, 2010).

111 John Dear, *The God of Peace: Toward a Theology of Nonviolence* (Eugene, OR: Wipf & Stock, 2008), 64.

peace in a permanent war economy."[112]

For the sake of partnerships, for project success, and for simply being better able to see clearly, it is critical for any social entrepreneur to constantly hone peacemaking skills. It begins with us.

EIGHTH BEATITUDE – PERSECUTED FOR RIGHTEOUSNESS' SAKE

The final Beatitude is cautionary. It advises that, rather than expecting laurels for your work, you may, in fact, be persecuted. If peacemaking, justice, or whatever other social justice goal you've set your heart on is elusive, and if people accuse you of having false motives, and if they attack you, it still is better that you continue on your path. This is the path many prophets have taken in the past. One needs to be meek and merciful and practice forgiveness precisely *because* there is no perfect justice, and it is illogical to expect it. And because your work is difficult and requires perseverance, it is important to cultivate a purity of heart, which will give you strength of conviction for your long, often solitary journey.

Jesus, at his crucifixion, was living out this Beatitude, and the ninth as well, "Blessed are you when people insult you, persecute you and falsely say all kinds of evil against you because of me. Rejoice and be glad, because great is your reward in heaven, for in the same way they persecuted the prophets who were before you." (Matthew, 5:11-12 NIV)

There is a poetic symmetry in the eighth Beatitude. First, we see the same closing promise as in the first Beatitude: the promise of the kingdom of heaven. Second, we see the same word as in the fourth Beatitude. In Greek, this is δικαιοσυνης, *dikaiosyne* (righteousness) and in Hebrew it is *haTs'daqah* (הַצְּדָקָה). Ending the first four Beatitudes, Jesus speaks of those blessed ones who

---

112 John Dear, *Jesus the Rebel; Bearer of God's Peace and Justice*, (Chicago, Ill: Sheed and Ward, 2000), 52.

continually hunger and thirst for righteousness. In the last four Beatitudes, he warns that this "blessed" road is not a garden path.

Too many people have misunderstood Jesus as glorifying suffering. Jesus was a realist. He knew the consequences of speaking truth to power and standing up for what is right. He also knew, and taught, a path to joy, right here and right now.

It is possible to feel peaceful and authentically joyful, right here and right now, when following this path with a whole heart, in spite of hostility and setbacks you may encounter in working for shalom-building. That is why, in the Gospel of John, Jesus is said to have told his disciples: "Peace I leave with you; my peace I give you. I do not give to you as the world gives. Do not let your hearts be troubled and do not be afraid." (John 14:27, NIV)

The key Greek and Hebrew words in the Beatitudes are persecuted (Greek: δεδιωγμενοι and Hebrew: *sheNir'd'phu* (שֶׁנִּרְדְּפוּ) and the reason for the persecution: righteousness' sake (Greek: δικαιοσυνης and Hebrew: *haTs'daqa*, (הַצְּדָקָה). It is interesting to note that although righteousness and justice have the same root in Hebrew, in the West we tend to distinguish our interpretations of the two, to favor a translation of righteousness because it can be more personally and individually applied. Non-Western commentators are more likely to translate it as justice because its application is more aligned with a community/systemic context.

Jesus appears to be saying that even if peace is elusive, and even if people accuse you of having false motives, and even if they attack you for following all the other Beatitudes, it still is better to pursue righteousness. After all, the Bible and post-biblical history are replete with examples of people paying the ultimate price for working to advance the greater good.

This Beatitude involves standing up for what is right, even when the consequences for doing so will be personally devastating. Many people will try for a time but will give up. They fall away as soon as their ego isn't satisfied with quick and easy results, and especially if they run into hardship or persecution. Jesus spoke of this, too, in his parable of the seed that landed on hard soil: "The seed falling on rocky ground refers to someone who hears the word and at once receives it with joy. But since they have no root, they last only a short time. When trouble or persecution comes because of the word, they quickly fall away." (Matthew 13:20-21, NIV)

The final Pillar, staying the course even when there are bumps in the road, speaks directly to this Beatitude. However, a demonstrated willingness to stay the course also strengthens partnerships. When we recognize and respect our mutual interdependence, we become more willing to take risks and suffer in the short term, for a greater long-term good.

We can be poor, mourn and be meek. Knowing that some things are beyond our own power to resolve, we remain ready for inspiration and valid perception. We can see what the real justice issues are, and be truly merciful, act with purity of heart as peacemakers, and be called children of God. What better plan for a social entrepreneur working for intelligence and compassion in action?

CARTER'S PERSPECTIVE ON PILLAR/BEATITUDE RELATIONSHIP

In our ongoing discussions while I was working on my dissertation, President Carter was extremely reluctant to compare his seven points to Jesus' eight Beatitudes, just as no humble artisan would wish to compare his product to that of a greater master artist. Referring to his Bible, he emphasized several times that while his own points are practical and achievable, "Jesus goes beyond that. He sets standards I don't think we can reach. Jesus paints a picture of human perfection. Love your enemies. You don't need to become a perfect person before you can love your neighbor, if you define your neighbor as lovable."

President Carter did confirm that he did not sit down one day and purposefully derive his Seven Pillars from the Beatitudes. Nor did he look at the Beatitudes and say, "These are for interior landscape building; mine are more practical." He would not knowingly create a system that is antithetical to Jesus' teachings either. He simply had not previously associated the two as systems.

President Carter, as a deacon of his church, is striving to be a disciple and follower of Jesus to the best of his abilities, and working actively to bring about a just peace long after most people would be resting on their laurels. His Seven Pillars seem to reflect his practical understanding of how to implement transformative leadership in uncharted territory, which he feels called to do as a follower of Jesus.

We met in early 2010 to discuss in detail The Carter Center's methodology. During our meeting, President Carter, who enjoys reading theology, was reading a biography of the great Lutheran martyr Dietrich Bonhoeffer, who plotted to kill Hitler in an attempt to save many more Jewish lives, and who was executed by the Nazis. We started out by discussing Bonhoeffer's rejection of what he called a false choice between cheap grace and legalism, and his embrace of "costly" grace.[113] We debated whether it is, as Bonhoeffer claimed, better to do evil than be evil, or whether we become the evil we hate in the process of taking up arms against evil. In the face of evil such as Hitler, do we turn the other cheek as Jesus instructs us, or do we act with evil means to destroy a greater evil? Carter told me, "We commit to peace as we worship the Prince of Peace."

The social entrepreneur's outlook or vision is also best when firmly grounded in solid bedrock teaching. To me, without such

---

113 Eric Metaxas, *Dietrich Bonhoeffer: Pastor, Martyr, Prophet, Spy.* Nashville, TN: Thomas Nelson, 2010.

grounding, one runs the danger of going off course, confusing personal aspirations for inspired vision. My personal choice is the Beatitudes for a true vision for peace and justice, building immunity to corrosive naysayers while still being able to humbly discern the voices of reason. In an imperfect world where absolute justice is unreachable, the Beatitudes cultivate mercy and purity of heart while counseling meekness. And they are realistic about the world's reaction.

ESSAY EXERCISE

1. *Print out the Beatitudes. Take a walk in a beautiful garden, along a coastal path or anywhere that brings you peace. Read the Beatitudes aloud. To find your necessary space – that empty spot in the puzzle where you fit – try to empty yourself of "self" and notice in what way you mourn the state of the world.*

2. *In what regard do you hunger and thirst for things to be more right? Consider how meekness, purity of heart, peacemaking and mercy might help you if you were to enter this space, addressing this need while not treading on other people's turf. Is there a need that calls to you? Are there reasons no one else seems to be addressing that need?*

ESSAY SET 3: THE PAYOFF

WHY FOLLOW THIS ROAD?

Understanding where and why you are called to action can be envisioned as a "lock for which you hold the key." The first three Pillars of the Seven Pillar methodology enable you to stay within your key abilities, putting your special skills to good use and filling a perceived chasm or void.

President Carter touches on this often in his writings. "All of us," he writes, "need to look at ourselves, our circumstances, the environment in which we live, and ask, 'Within my own talent and realm of possibilities, what can I find to do that would be good and lovely?'[114]

"As we expand our lives and do things that are challenging, innovative, and unpredictable, we can know what it means to be filled with joy and the peace that passes understanding."[115]

Activist and author of *Life Is a Contact Sport*, Ken Kragen, in giving life wisdom, advises us to stay where our skills and our affinities intersect. But once, visiting The Carter Center, staffer Gabrielle Mertz, echoing President Carter's advice, reminded me to consider a third factor when choosing our life's work: the world's deep needs. Finding a chasm to fill, after all, is one of the seven pillars. This three-pronged advice echoes Frederick Buechner, who said your *vocation* is that place where your deep gladness and the world's greatest needs converge.[116] Mertz suggests that this could be well represented in a Venn diagram, but I would envision these

---

114 Jimmy Carter, *Living Faith* (New York, NY: Random House, 1996), 255.

115 Ibid., 256.

116 Bob Abernathy. "Profile: Frederick Buechner" *Religion & Ethics Newsweekly*, May 5, 2006. Episode. 936. http://www.pbs.org/wnet/religionandethics/week936/profile.html (accessed June 28, 2012).

three factors as a three dimensional cube, perhaps represented in slices, or as an exploded box:

ILLUSTRATION: THE "RUBRIC CUBE"

ILLUSTRATION: THINK IN AN OPEN OR EXPLODED BOX

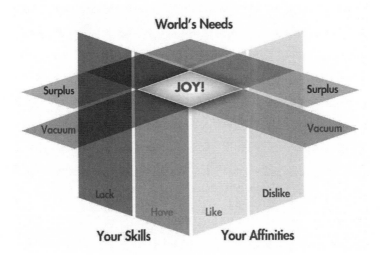

The above illustrations show the intersection where your affinities and your skills align with the world's needs, and joy is found.

When I am asked to sit on a board, I consider how effective I will be as a member. I also weigh whether my own particular skills are relevant. Knowing my affinities helps me make better decisions with my limited time. It can be the same, for you.

ESSAY QUESTIONS

1. *Draw a three-part Venn Diagram. Label one part "world's needs," another "my skills" and another "my passions." Consider where all three intersect.*

2. *Create a square. Label one side "my skills/lacks" and the other side "enjoy /don't enjoy." Consider the advice about how the world will pull you into areas you don't enjoy, but for which you have skills. What does this mean for your own life?*

BIBLIOGRAPHY AND APPENDICES

APPENDIX A: BEATITUDES IN ENGLISH, ARAMAIC, HEBREW AND GREEK

[Matthew 5:3-10. English; Aramaic interlinear; Hebrew interlinear and text (right to left); Greek]

1. **ENGLISH**: 3 *Blessed are the humble of spirit for theirs is the kingdom of heaven.*

    ARAMAIC: (in The Spirit) ברוח (who are poor) למכנא (blessed are they) טוביהון (of Heaven) דסמיא (the Kingdom) מלכותא (is) הי (because theirs) דדילהון

    HEBREW: הַשָּׁמַיִם [אַשְׁרֵי עֲנִיֵי רוּח כִּי שֶׁלָהֶם הִיא מַלְכוּת הַשָּׁמַיִם (haShamayim$_{8064}$ - heavens) / מַלְכוּת (Malkhut$_{4438}$ - realm) / הִיא (Hi$_{1931}$ – that) / שֶׁלָהֶם (shelaHem$_{1992}$ - the same) / כִּי (Ki$_{3588}$ – for) / רוּח (ruach$_{7307}$– breath/spirit/mind) / עֲנִיֵי (aniyei$_{6041}$ - poor, afflicted, humble, wretched, lowly) / אַשְׁרֵי (Ashrei$_{835}$ – blessed)]. *Pronounce: Ashrei aniyei ruach ki shelachem hi malkhut hashamayim.*

    GREEK:$_{3}$μακαριοι οι πτωχοι τω πνευματι οτι αυτων εστιν η βασιλεια των ουρανων [poor in spirit: πτωχοι – ptochoi (Strongs 4434)].

2. **ENGLISH**:4 *Blessed are those who mourn, for they shall be comforted.*

    ARAMAIC: (will be comforted) נתביאונ (for they) דהנונ (who are mourning) לאבילא (blessed are they) טוביהונ

HEBREW: יִנָּחֵמוּ הֵם כִּי הָאֲבֵלִים אַשְׁרֵי [יְנֻחָמוּ (*Y'nuchamu*$_{5162}$ – to be consoled) / הֵם (*Hem*$_{1992}$ – these same) / כִּי (*Ki*$_{3588}$ – for) / הָאֲבֵלִים (*ha'avelim*$_{56/8802}$ – those who mourn) / אַשְׁרֵי (*Ashrei*$_{835}$ – blessed)]. *Pronounce: Ashrei ha'avelim ki hem y'nuchamu.*

GREEK:$_4$ μακαριοι οι πενθουντες οτι αυτοι παρακληθησονται [mourn: πενθουντες – penthountes (Strongs 3996)].

3. **ENGLISH**: 5 *Blessed are the meek, for they will inherit the earth.*

ARAMAIC: (the earth) לארא (will inherit) Nwtran (for they) דהנונג (who are meek) למכיכא (blessed are they) טוביהון

HEBREW: הָאָרֶץ [אַשְׁרֵי הָעֲנָוִים כִּי הֵם יִירְאוּ אֶת הָאָרֶץ (*haArets*$_{776}$ – earth) / אֶת (*Et*$_{853}$ – definitive direct object) / יִירְאוּ (*Yir'u*$_{3423/8799}$ –) / הֵם (*Hem*$_{1992}$ – these same)/ כִּי (*Ki*$_{3588}$ – for) / הָעֲנָוִים (*ha'anavim*$_{6035}$ – humble, lowly, meek, poor) / אַשְׁרֵי (*Ashrei*$_{835}$ – blessed)]. *Pronounce: Ashrei ha'anavim ki hem yir'u et ha'aretz.*

GREEK:$_5$ μακαριοι οι πραεις οτι αυτοι κληρονομησουσιν την γην [meekness: πραεις – praus (Strongs 4239)].

4. **ENGLISH**: 6 *Blessed are those who hunger and thirst for righteousness; they will be filled.*

ARAMAIC: (who hunger) דכפנינ (those) לאילינ (blessed are they) טוביהונ (will be satisfied) נבונ (for they) דהנונג (for justice) לכאנותא (& thirst) והינ

HEBREW: יִשְׂבָּעוּ [אַשְׁרֵי הָרְעֵבִים וּצְמֵאִים לַצְּדָקָה כִּי הֵם יִשְׂבָּעוּ (*Yis'b'u*$_{7646\ (8799)}$ – will be sated) / הֵם (*Hem*$_{1992}$ – these same) / כִּי (*Ki*$_{3588}$ – for) / לַצְּדְקָה (*laTs'daqah*$_{6666}$ – for righteousness) / וּצְמֵאִים (*uTs'me'im*$_{6770}$ – those who thirst) / הָרְעֵבִים

(*haR'evim*$_{7457\,(8802)}$ – those who hunger) / אַשְׁרֵי (*Ashrei*$_{835}$ – blessed)]. *Pronounce: Ashrei haR'evim uTs'me'im laTs'daqah ki hem Yis'b'u.*

GREEK:$_6$μακαριοι οι πεινωντες και διψωντες την δικαιοσυνην οτι αυτοι χορτασθησονται [hunger πεινάω peinaó (Strongs 3983); διψωντες dipsaóntes, (Strongs 1372); righteousness: δικαιοσυνην – dikaiosuné (Strongs 1343)].

5. **ENGLISH**: 7 *Blessed are the merciful, for they will be shown mercy.*

ARAMAIC: (who show mercy) למרחמנא (blessed are they) דליהון (for upon them)) נהוון (there will be) רחמא (mercies) טוביהון

HEBREW: רַחֲמִים [אַשְׁרֵי הָרַחֲמָנִים כִּי עֲלֵיהֶם יִהְיוּ רַחֲמִים (*Rachamim*$_{7356}$– mercy, tender love, compassion) / יִהְיוּ (*Yihyu*$_{1961\,(8799)}$ – come to pass) / עֲלֵיהֶם (*Aleyhem*$_{5921}$ – upon) / כִּי (*Ki*$_{3588}$ – for) / הָרַחֲמָנִים (*haRachamanim*$_{7355\,(8764)}$ – those who show compassion / mercy) / אַשְׁרֵי (*Ashrei*$_{835}$ – blessed)]. *Pronounce: Ashrei haRachamanim ki aleihem yihyu.*

GREEK:$_7$μακαριοι οι ελεημονες οτι αυτοι ελεηθησονται [merciful: ελεημονες eleēmones (Strongs 1655)].

6. **ENGLISH**: 8 *Blessed are the innocent of heart for they shall see God.*

ARAMAIC: (in their hearts) בלבהון (who are pure) דדכין (those) לאילין (blessed are they) טוביהון (God) לאלהא (shall see) נחזון (for they) דהנונ

HEBREW: הָאֱלֹהִים [אַשְׁרֵי הַטְּהוֹרִים בִּלְבָבָם אֶת יִרְשָׁאוּ הָאֱלֹהִים (*haElohim*$_{430}$ - God) / יִרְשָׁאוּ (*Yirshu*$_{7200?}$ –see) / אֶת (*Et*$_{853}$ – not generally translated) / בִּלְבָבָם (*biL'vavam*$_{3824}$ – heart, moral

character, inner man, mind, will, heart, soul, understanding)
/ הַטְּהוֹרִים ($haT'horim_{2889}$ – clean) / אַשְׁרֵי ($Ashrei_{835}$ – blessed)].
Pronounce: Ashrei haT'horim biL'vavam et haElohim.

GREEK:$_8$μακαριοι οι καθαροι τη καρδια οτι αυτοι τον θεον
οψονται [pure: καθαροι , katharoi (Strongs 2513) ; heart:
καρδια, kardia, (Strongs 2588)].

7. **ENGLISH**: 9 *Blessed are those who pursue peace for they*
shall be called children of God.

ARAMAIC: (peace) סלמא (that make) לבדי (blessed are they)
טוביהון (they will be called) נתקרון (of God) דאלהא (for the
children) דבנוהי

HEBREW: יִקָּרְאוּ] אַשְׁרֵי עוֹשֵׂי שָׁלוֹם כִּי בְנֵי אֱלֹהִים יִקָּרְאוּ.
($Yiqar'u_{7121}$ – will be called) / אֱלֹהִים ($Elohim_{430}$ - God) / בְּנֵי
($B'nei11_{21}$ – children)/ כִּי (Ki_{3588} – for) / שָׁלוֹם ($Shalom_{7965}$
- peace) / עוֹשֵׂי ($Osei_{6213}$ – bringers of) / אַשְׁרֵי ($Ashrei_{835}$ –
blessed)]. *Pronounce: Ashrei osei shalom ki b'nei Elohim*
yiqar'u.

GREEK:$_9$μακαριοι οι ειρηνοποιοι οτι αυτοι υιοι θεου
κληθησονται [peacemaker: ειρηνοποιοι, eirénopoioi (Strongs
1518)].

8. **ENGLISH**: 10 *Blessed are those persecuted for righteousness,*
for theirs is the kingdom of heaven.

ARAMAIC: (for the cause of) מטל (who have been persecuted)
דאתרדפו (those) לאילין (blessed are they) טוביהון (of Heaven)
דסמיא (the Kingdom) מלכותא (is) הי (for theirs) דדילהון (justice)
כאנותא.

HEBREW: שֶׁנֶּרְדְּפוּ בִּגְלַל הַצְּדָקָה כִּי שֶׁלָּהֶם הִיא מַלְכוּת הַשָּׁמַיִם

אַשְׁרֵי הַלָּלוּ [הַשָּׁמַיִם (*haShamayim*₈₀₆₄ - heavens) / מַלְכוּת
(*Malkhut*₄₄₃₈ - realm) / הִיא (*Hi*₁₉₃₁ – that) / שֶׁלָּהֶם (*shelaHem*₁₉₉₂
- these same) / כִּי (*Ki*₃₅₈₈ – for) / הַצְּדָקָה (*haTs'daqah*₆₆₆₆ – from
tzedek righteousness) / בִּגְלַל (*biG'lal*₁₅₅₈ – over circumstance
of) / שֶׁנִּרְדְּפוּ (*sheNir'd'phu*₇₂₉₁ - persecute, chase) / הַלָּלוּ (*haLalu*₀
- those) / אַשְׁרֵי (*Ashrei*₈₃₅ – blessed)]. *Pronounce: Ashrei haLalu
shenir'd'phu big'lal hats'daqah ki shelahem hi malkhut
haShamayim.*

GREEK:₁₀μακαριοι οι δεδιωγμενοι ενεκεν δικαιοσυνης οτι
αυτων εστιν η βασιλεια των ουρανων [persecute: δεδιωγμενοι,
dediōgmenoi (Strongs 1377); righteousness δικαιοσυνης,
dikaiosonais (Strongs 1343)].

APPENDIX B: SELECTED CONTACT INFORMATION

Access to Capital for Entrepreneurs
www.aceloans.org
3173 U.S. 129 / Cleveland, GA 30528-2715
(706) 348-6609 info@aceloans.org
Access to Capital for Entrepreneurs (ACE), formerly Appalachian
Community Enterprises, is an SBA Microloan Intermediary and
certified Community Development Financial Institution (CDFI)
founded in 1998. Since that time, ACE has provided over $4 million
in financing to small businesses. Through loans, financial literacy
education, coaching and connections, ACE has helped hundreds of
north Georgians fulfill their dreams.

The All Stars Project of the San Francisco/Bay Area
www.allstarsproject.org
870 Market Street, Suite 841 / San Francisco, CA 94102
(415) 986-2502
The All Stars Project of the San Francisco Bay Area is part of All
Stars Project, Inc a national nonprofit promoting human development
through an innovative performance-based model, with outside-of-
school, educational and performing arts activities for thousands of
poor and minority young people. The organization develops leadership
training and pursues volunteer initiatives that build and strengthen
communities. The ASP actively promotes supplementary education
and the performance-learning model in academic and civic arena.
SF Bay Area Director Joyce Dattner is a recipient of the Elfenworks
Foundation *In Harmony with Hope* award.

AmpleHarvest.org
www.ampleharvest.org
24 Clover Rd / Newfoundland, NJ 07435
267-536-9880 (AMPLE-6-9880) info@ampleharvest.org
AmpleHarvest.org is a nationwide campaign to enable America's 40+

million home gardeners who grow food to be able to easily share some of their harvest with local food pantries. At its core is a web portal, connecting enrolled food pantries with gardeners nearby. Founder Gary Oppenheimer is a CNN Hero and a recipient of the Elfenworks Foundation *In Harmony with Hope* award.

Boys Hope Girls Hope
www.boyshopegirlshope.org
12120 Bridgeton Square Drive / Bridgeton, MO 63044
(314) 298-1250; 877-878-HOPE; Fax 314-298-1251; hope@bhgh.org
Boys Hope Girls Hope helps academically capable and motivated children-in-need to meet their full potential through opportunities and education through college and become young men and women for others. CEO Paul Minorini is a recipient of the Elfenworks Foundation *In Harmony with Hope* award.

Campus MovieFest
www.campusmoviefest.com
info@campusmoviefest.com
The world's largest student film festival and a premier outlet for the next generation of filmmakers. CMF provides students with everything they need to make movies in one week. CMF is free to students thanks to corporate partners and schools. In partnership with The Elfenworks Foundation, CMF provides the farthest reaching student social justice media award, the Elfenworks Social Justice Prize.

Capuchin Soup Kitchen
www.cskdetroit.org
1820 Mt. Elliott Street / Detroit, MI 48207
(313) 579-2100 ext. 215 *www.cskdetroit.org/contact.cfm#feedback*
The Capuchin Soup Kitchen provides far more than simple material assistance, as it also—and perhaps more importantly—acts as a healing force in the spirits and lives of the individuals it serves. The CSK works to restore self-esteem, motivation, and meaning. The Capuchin

Soup Kitchen was featured in the film *Faces of Poverty*, produced by
The San Damiano Foundation in association with The Elfenworks
Foundation. Scenes show the steps taken to provide new skills, helping
to restore independence and dignity.

The Carter Center
www.cartercenter.org
One CopenHill, 453 Freedom Parkway / Atlanta GA 30307
(404) 420-5100
The Carter Center is committed to advancing human rights and
alleviating unnecessary human suffering. They invite you to join
them in creating a world in which every man, woman, and child has
the opportunity to enjoy good health and live in peace. Co-founder
Rosalynn Carter is a recipient of The Elfenworks Foundation *In
Harmony with Hope* award.

Center for Science in the Public Interest
www.cspinet.org
1220 L Street, NW, Suite 300 / Washington, D.C. 20005
(202) 777-8328/ cspi@cspinet.org
A strong advocate for nutrition and health, food safety, alcohol policy,
and sound science since 1971, The Center for Science in the Public
Interest also boasts the largest-circulation health newsletter in North
America, the award-winning *Nutrition Action Healthletter*. Founded
by Executive Director Michael Jacobson, Ph.D. and two other
scientists.

Center on Poverty & Inequality at Stanford University
www.inequality.com
Building 80, 450 Serra Mall, Stanford, CA 94305-2029
(650) 724-6912 / inequality@stanford.edu
This center's objectives include supporting scientific analysis of
poverty and inequality, developing science-based policy on poverty
and inequality, disseminating data and research on poverty and

inequality, and training the next generation of scholars, policy analysts, and politicians. Center founded by director Dr. David Grusky, who can be seen on the Elfenworks feature film *The Concert for Hope*.

Children of the Night
www.childrenofthenight.org
14530 Sylvan Street / Van Nuys, California 91411
Hotline: (800) 551-1300 / Main: (818) 908-4474 / llee@ childrenofthenight.org Children of the Night is dedicated to assisting children between the ages of 11 and 17 who are forced to prostitute on the streets for food to eat and a place to sleep. Donations are welcome and needed, and a wish list is kept updated, on the website. Founder Lois Lee is a recipient of an Elfenworks *In Harmony with Hope* award.

Common Ground
www.commonground.org
505 Eighth Avenue, 15th Floor / New York, NY 10018
212-389-9300 / info@commonground.org
Common Ground was a pioneer in the development of supportive housing and other research-based practices that end homelessness. Common Ground's network of well-designed, affordable apartments— linked to the services people need to maintain their housing, restore their health, and regain their economic independence—has helped thousands to overcome homelessness. Founder Rosanne Haggerty is a recipient of an Elfenworks *In Harmony with Hope* award.

College Possible
www.collegepossible.org
450 N Syndicate Street, Suite 325 / Saint Paul, MN 55104
(651) 917-3525 info@CollegePossible.org
College Possible's goal is to make postsecondary education a reality for the 200,000 at-risk kids each year who graduate high school prepared for college but who, thanks to cultural and functional barriers, aren't able to get there. College Possible delivers highly personalized

support to its 9,000 low-income students annually in the Twin Cities area, Milwaukee, and, starting this year, in Omaha, Nebraska. They are in the process of scaling up to serve 20,000 students annually across the country in the next several years. Founder Jim McCorkell, an Ashoka Fellow, is a recipient of the Elfenworks *In Harmony with Hope* award, among many other accolades. He was the first person in the country to leverage the AmeriCorps service infrastructure for college access, and it is essential to the model's success.

Communities In Schools

www.communitiesinschools.org

2345 Crystal Drive, Suite 801 / Arlington, VA 22202

703-519-8999 / info@cisnet.org

Communities In Schools, the country's largest dropout prevention network, was founded on the principle that programs don't change kids but relationships do. For more than 30 years, CIS has developed effective community partnerships between schools, families, and community leaders to build a solid support system for students. The organization directly serves more than 1.3 million students and their families each year in over 3,000 schools in 26 states and the District of Columbia. Founder Bill Milliken, who has served three U.S. Presidents, is the recipient of an *In Harmony with Hope* award, as well as the National Jefferson Award for Public Service.

Community Solutions

www. cmtysolutions.org

14 E. 28th St, PH, New York, NY 10016

212.471.0800 info@cmtysolutions.org

Community Solutions is spreading the work begun by founder Rosanne Haggerty at Common Ground to cities across the nation and worldwide. Community Solutions' 100,000 homes campaign has a nationwide goal: collectively house 100,000 of the nation's most homeless individuals and families by July, 2014. It works to achieve that goal by coordinating national organizations and local community efforts. Founder Rosanne Haggerty is a recipient of an Elfenworks *In Harmony with Hope* award.

D.C. Central Kitchen
www.dccentralkitchen.org
425 2nd Street, NW/ Washington, DC 20001-2003
(202) 234-0707 www.dccentralkitchen.org/contact.php
Through job training, meal distribution, and supporting local food systems, DC Central Kitchen is building long-term solutions to the interconnected problems of poverty, hunger, and homelessness. The Kitchen is founded on the premise that when fighting poverty, one must fight to win by using every resource available: "Be it food, money, or people, we hate to see wasted potential." Founder Robert Egger is a recipient of the Elfenworks Foundation's *In Harmony with Hope* award.

The Elfenworks Foundation
www.elfenworks.org
20 Park Road, Suite D / Burlingame, CA 94010
650 347 9700 – elfenworks@elfenworks.org
The Elfenworks Foundation's mission is to foster a world *In Harmony with Hope*® by working for hope in America, one good thought at a time. Our vision for achieving our mission is to innovate and bridge-build for a better tomorrow. Working in partnership, we value intelligent compassion in action.

Family Independence Initiative
www.fiinet.org
1203 Preservation Park Way, Suite 100 / Oakland, CA 94612
(510) 452-9341
The Family Independence Initiative (FII) is a national center for innovating new strength-based approaches for economic and social mobility. FII operates under the assumption that most low-income families are capable of taking tangible steps towards establishing

control and choice in their lives. Since 2001 FII has been partnering with low-income families to show that investing in their strengths and initiative delivers more powerful, sustainable, and cost effective outcomes. President and Founder Maurice Lim Miller was appointed by President Obama to serve on the White House Council for Community Solutions, and is a recipient of an Elfenworks *In Harmony with Hope* award.

Generations of Hope Development Corporation
generationsofhope.org
409 Devonshire Drive / Champaign, IL 61820
(217) 363-3080 ghdc@generationsofhope.org
Generations of Hope's model is of an intentional intergenerational village filled with parents raising and adopting foster children and senior citizens volunteering to help support the kids and the community, in exchange for lowered rents. Hope Meadows opened on a closed military base in Illinois in 1994, and now a dozen families live in the community, free of rent. In exchange, they agree to adopt three or four foster care system children who have slim chances of finding permanent homes. Those children, once the most difficult to place, boast a high 89% permanency rate. Founder Brenda Krause Eheart, PhD, is the recipient of an Elfenworks *In Harmony with Hope* award.

Genesys Works
www.genesysworks.org
2800 Post Oak Blvd., Suite 6200 / Houston, TX 77056
(713) 341-0522 ~ info@genesysworks.org
Genesys Works changes the trajectory of life for underprivileged students by providing them a meaningful internship during their senior year in high school. After an initial eight-week intensive training on technical and soft-skills, students are assigned to work in a year-long internship at one of over a hundred participating corporations. As a true social enterprise, three quarters of their budget is provided by partner companies, who benefit by engaging their trained "young

professionals" at below-market rates. As students recognize their potential as professionals in the corporate world, their future is forever changed. More than 95% of graduates go on to college, and over 70% persist in their college career. Founder Rafael Alvarez is a recipient of an Elfenworks *In Harmony with Hope* award.

Golden Gate University School of Law
www.ggu.edu
Elfenworks Center for Employment Justice at the Graduate School of Law – *www.law.ggu.edu/law/werc*
536 Mission Street / San Francisco, CA 94105
(415) 442-7820 / lawcareer@ggu.edu
Golden Gate University School of Law is committed to making a positive and lasting impact on poverty law and human rights by providing high-quality, skills-infused education designed to enhance social and economic justice, including via ground-breaking advocacy in the area of domestic workers rights, and transformational scholarship and national collaborations in the field of poverty law via such events such as the GGU/Society of American Law Teachers 2010 Conference on "Vulnerable Populations and Economic Realities" and the resultant publication, Vulnerable Populations and Transformative Teaching: A Critical Reader.

Growing Power
www.growingpower.org
5500 West Silver Spring Drive / Milwaukee, WI 53218-3261
(414) 527-1546 / staff@growingpower.org
From a 2.5-acre farm, located in the heart of Milwaukee, Growing Power is bringing healthy, low-cost, sustainable food to the "food deserts" of our nation's urban centers, while educating a nation of the benefits of urban farming, and mitigating racism by empowering the minority communities they serve. Growing Power also runs numerous collaborative projects, teen internships and training projects, which engage city youth in producing healthy foods for their communities.

Founder Will Allen –named by Time Magazine as one of the World's 100 Most Influential People – is a McArthur Fellow, a member of the Clinton Global Initiative, and recipient of an Elfenworks *In Harmony with Hope* award.

Health Leads
www.healthleadsusa.org
2 Oliver Street, 10th Floor / Boston, MA 02109
(617) 391-3633 / national@healthleadsusa.org
By enabling doctors to write prescriptions to fill their patients' basic resource needs, Health Leads envisions a healthcare system that addresses all patients' basic resource needs as a standard part of quality care. Health Leads connects patients with the basic resources they need to be healthy, and in doing so, builds leaders with the conviction and ability to champion quality care for all patients. For her model of health care delivery, founder Rebecca Onie is a recipient of an Elfenworks *In Harmony with Hope* award.

Homeboy Industries
www.homeboy-industries.org
130 W. Bruno St / Los Angeles, CA 90012
(323) 526-1254 / info@homeboy-industries.org
Homeboy Industries uses a "jobs not jails" intelligent, compassionate approach to assist at-risk and formerly gang-involved youth to become positive and contributing members of society through job placement, training and education. Founder Greg Boyle, SJ is a recipient of an Elfenworks *In Harmony with Hope* award.

Lasallian Volunteers of the De La Salle Christian Brothers
www.lasallianvolunteers.org
Hecker Center, Suite 300 / 3025 Fourth St., NE / Washington, DC 20017 (202) 529-0047
The Lasallian Volunteers (a program of the De La Salle Brothers of the Christian Schools Region of North America) provides dedicated,

well-trained volunteers for one or more years of service to schools
and agencies of the Brothers whose mission is to serve the poor.
Acting out of faith, rooted in the Gospel, and sharing community
with the Brothers and other Lasallians, the volunteers empower the
poor by personalized service primarily through education. The film,
LVs Ride, produced in partnership with Campus Moviefest, The
Elfenworks Foundation, and The San Damiano Foundation, illustrates
how Lasallian Volunteers change the world for the better and discover
themselves transformed in the process.

MicroVest

www.microvestfund.com

7315 Wisconsin Avenue, Suite 300W / Bethesda, MD 20814

(301) 664-6680 / info@microvestfund.com

MicroVest is a microfinance investment firm providing capital and
management oversight, believes another asset is a mindset that enables
risk-taking when there is a potential for high rewards.

Mills College of California

www.mills.edu & *www.mills.edu/mba/*

5000 MacArthur Blvd. / Oakland, CA 94613

510.430.2255 / csrb@mills.edu

For more than 150 years Mills College has served as a pioneer in
teaching women to be socially responsible, innovative, and creative
leaders in society. Mills undergraduate women are well known for
their commitment to justice, their interest in international affairs, their
activism on behalf of others, etc. The Center for Socially Responsible
Business, supported by The Elfenworks Foundation, examines how
businesses can improve social conditions in practical ways, ways that
do not harm—and may even help—their bottom lines. Businesses
can flourish financially by doing good, socially.

One Million Lights

www.onemillionlights.org

(650) 387-3150 / contact@onemillionlights.org

When the sun sets every day, millions of homes around the world go into darkness. In the 21st century, we should be able to offer a clean and eco-friendly solution. The vision: to improve the daily lives of children and adults by providing one million clean and healthy solar lights to families around the world which replace toxic kerosene lamps and enable children to study at night. Founder Anna Sidana and OML also work with local schools to increase awareness of global issues.

Partners in Health

www.pih.org

888 Commonwealth Avenue, 3rd Floor / Boston, MA 02215

(617) 998-8922 / info@pih.org

Founded in 1987, Partners in Health is a nonprofit organization relentlessly committed to improving the health of the poor and marginalized. As of 2012, PIH employs nearly 13,000 people and works in 76 health centers and hospitals in 10 countries. Their work follows five principles: providing universal access to primary health care; making health care and education free to the poor; hiring and training community health workers; fighting poverty in order to fight disease; partnering with local and national governments. PIH is based in Boston and also serves a small population living with HIV/AIDS and diabetes there. Co-founder Dr. Paul Farmer is a recipient of an Elfenworks *In Harmony with Hope* award.

Peter Young Housing, Industries & Treatment

www.pyhit.com

Donations: The Peter G Young Foundation, 40 Eagle Street / Albany, NY 12207

(518) 463-8485

A simple three-legged stool is the symbol of Rev. Peter Young's lifetime of work, and he uses it to explain his successful model for rehabilitating addicts. The three requirements for success at PYHITare treatment, housing and employment. Donations of any kind are welcome. Rev. Peter Young is a recipient of an Elfenworks *In Harmony with Hope* award.

St. Francis Inn

www.stfrancisinn.org

2441 Kensington Ave / Philadelphia, PA 19125

(215) 423-5845

The St. Francis Inn of Philadelphia is a Franciscan community located in the Kensington neighborhood of Philadelphia. Their community is composed of religious and lay people who live and minister among the poor and homeless. They seek to empower persons to break the cycle of homelessness and poverty and address structural injustices. The St. Francis Inn was featured in the film *Faces of Poverty*, produced by The San Damiano Foundation in association with The Elfenworks Foundation.

Saint Mary's College of California

www.stmarys-ca.edu

Elfenworks Center for the Study of Fiduciary Capitalism – *www. fidcap.org*

Catholic Institute for Lasallian Social Action

www.stmarys-ca.edu/academics/cilsa/

1928 Saint Mary's Road / Moraga, CA 94575

Saint Mary's College of California is a Lasallian liberal arts college with a strong commitment to service and social justice. Fidcap.org leads the discussion at the intersection between corporate governance and fiduciary institutions. CILSA, Catholic Institute for Lasallian Social Action, promotes, organizes, and supports service on behalf of social justice by members of the Saint Mary's community.

Sustainable Conservation

www.suscon.org

98 Battery St # 302 San Francisco, CA 94111

(415) 977-0380 / suscon@suscon.org

Sustainable Conservation believes protecting the environment can also be good for business, and advances the stewardship of natural resources using innovative, pragmatic strategies that actively engage businesses and private landowners in conservation. Founded in 1993, Sustainable Conservation's effectiveness lies in building strong partnerships with business, agriculture and government – and establishing models for environmental and economic sustainability that can be replicated across California and beyond.

UCSF Center for Vulnerable Populations

http://cvp.ucsf.edu

Center for Vulnerable Populations / 1001 Potrero Ave, Building 10, Ward 13 / San Francisco, CA 94110. / San Francisco, CA 94110. Center Contact: Purba Chatterjee, MPH, Center Manager / Bldg 90, 1st Floor San Francisco General Hospital / 995 Portrero Avenue, Rm 128 / San Francisco CA 94110. (415) 206-5277 / chatterjeep@medsfgh.ucsf.edu

The UCSF Center for Vulnerable Populations (CVP) at San Francisco General Hospital and Trauma Center is dedicated to improving health and reducing disparities through discovery, innovation, policy, advocacy, and community partnerships. The CVP seeks to develop effective strategies to prevent and treat chronic diseases in communities most at risk. The Elfenworks Foundation provided assistance to the Center, in creating its web presence.

Union Rescue Mission

www.urm.org

545 South San Pedro Street, Los Angeles, CA 90013

(213) 347-6300 thewayhome@urm.org

The Union Rescue Mission provides shelter and addiction treatment facilities in the Los Angeles skid row area. Its activities and facilities were depicted in the film *Faces of Poverty*, produced by The San Damiano Foundation in association with The Elfenworks Foundation.

Universal Health Care Action Network
www.uhcan.org
2800 Euclid Avenue, 520 / Cleveland, OH 44115-2418
(216) 241-8422 / uhcan@uhcan.org
The Universal Health Care Action Network (UHCAN) is a national network that connects groups working for health care justice around multiple approaches and with diverse constituencies in states and nationally so as to promote information-sharing, best practices and collaboration. Rachel Rosen DeGolia, Director.

Volunteers in Medicine
www.volunteersinmedicine.org
162 St. Paul Street / Burlington, VT 05401
(802) 651-0112 / info@vimi.org
The motto of VIM: "A National Solution to America's Uninsured, One Community at a Time." Many of the hundreds of thousands of retired physicians, nurses and dentists in the United States welcome the opportunity to enrich their retirement years by volunteering their skills on a part-time basis on behalf of the more than 41 million Americans who have no health insurance. Founder Dr. Jack McConnell is a recipient of an Elfenworks *In Harmony with Hope* award.

SELECTED BIBLIOGRAPHY

Abernathy, Bob. "Profile: Frederick Buechner" *Religion & Ethics Newsweekly,* May 5, 2006. Episode. 936. http://www.pbs.org/wnet/religionandethics/week936/profile.html (accessed June 28, 2012).

Amrine, Michael. "The Real Problem is in the Hearts of Men." *New York Times Magazine.* June 23, 1946.

Ariail, Dan, and Cheryl Heckler-Feltz. *The Carpenter's Apprentice: The Spiritual Biography of Jimmy Carter.* Grand Rapids, MI: Zondervan Publishing, 1996.

Bakke, Raymond J. *A Theology as Big as the City.* Downers Grove, IL: InterVarsity Press, 1997.

Banerjee, Abhijit Vinayak, with Alice Amsden, Robert Bates, Jagdish Bhagwati, Angus Deaton, Nicholas Stern and others. *Making Aid Work.* Cambridge, MA: MIT Press, 2007.

Barclay, William. *The Gospel of Matthew Volume One.* Rev. ed. Philadelphia, PA: Westminster Press, 1975.

Barenblat, Rachel. "The Velveteen Rabbi's Haggadah for Pesach, Version 5.0." http://www.velveteenrabbi.com/VRHaggadah.pdf (accessed June 10, 2010).

Bauscher, David. *The Aramaic-English Interlinear Gospels.* Raleigh, NC: Lulu Publishing, 2006.

Benioff, Mark, and Carlyle Adler. *The Business of Changing the World; Twenty Great Leaders on Strategic Corporate Philanthropy.* New York, NY: McGraw Hill, 2007.

BibleGateway.com, "1894 Scrivener New Testament," http://www.biblegateway.com/passage/?search=percentCEpercent9Apercentage=percentCEpercent91percentCEpercentA4percentCEpercent91percent20percentCEpercent9CpercentCEpercent91percentCEpercentA4percentCEpercent98percentCEpercent91percentCEpercent99percentCEpercent9FpercentCEpercent9Dpercent205&version=TR1894 (accessed June 3, 2010).

BibleGateway.com, "1550 Stephanus New Testament," http://www. biblegateway.com/passage/?search=Matthewpercent205.,perce nt203-10&version=TR1550 (accessed April 17, 2010).

BibleGateway.com "1881 Westcort-Hort New Testament," http://www. biblegateway.com/passage/?search=Matthewpercent205.,perce nt203-10&version=WHNU (accessed April 17, 2010).

Bill, J. Brent. *Sacred Compass: The Way of Spiritual Discernment.* Brewster, MA: Paraclete Press, 2008.

Block, Peter. *Stewardship: Choosing Service Over Self-Interest.* San Francisco, CA: Berrett-Koehler, 1993.

Bnei Baruch Kabbalah Education & Research Institute. "Racist Hate on the Rise in America." http://www.kabbalahblog.info/2008/07/ racist-hate-on-the-rise-in-america/ (accessed April 19, 2010).

Boice, James Montgomery. *The Sermon on the Mount; Matthew 5-7, An Expositional Commentary.* Grand Rapids, MI: Baker Books, 1972.

Bonhoeffer, Dietrich. *Discipleship.* Minneapolis, MN: Fortress Press. 2003.

Bornstein, David. *How to Change the World: Social Entrepreneurs and the Power of New Ideas.* Updated Ed. New York, NY: Oxford University Press, 2007.

B'rit Chadasah. "Matthew." http://www.britchadashah.net/chapter_ mat_5_hebrewenglish.html (accessed April 17, 2010).

Brooks, Arthur. *Social Entrepreneurship: A Modern Approach to Social Value Creation,* New York, NY: Prentice Hall, 2008.

Brueggemann, Walter. *Living Toward a Vision: Biblical Reflections on Shalom.* Cleveland, OH: United Church Press, 1982.

Campus MovieFest. "Home Page." http://www.campusmoviefest.com/ (accessed March 1, 2010).

Cantalamessa, Raniero, and Marsha Daigle-Williamson. *Beatitudes: Eight Steps to Happiness.* Cincinnati, OH: Servant Books, 2009.

The Carter Center. "2008-2009 Annual Report." www.cartercenter. org/news/publications/annual_reports.html (accessed March 27, 2011).

———. "The Carter Center China Program." http://www.cartercenter. org/peace/china_elections/index.html (accessed March 7, 2010).

———. "The Carter Center Democracy Program." http//www.carter-center.org/peace/democracy/index.html (accessed March 7, 2010).

———. "Guinea Worm Eradication Program." http://www.cartercenter. org/health/guinea_worm/index.html (accessed February 9, 2010).

———. "The Carter Center Trachoma Control Program." http://www. cartercenter.org/health/trachoma/index.html (accessed February 9, 2010).

———. "The Carter Center "Notable Achievements" Wall Exhibit. Atlanta, GA, The Carter Center Museum and Library. Visited February, 2010.

Carter, Jimmy. *Beyond the White House: Waging Peace, Fighting Disease, Building Hope.* New York, NY: Simon & Schuster, 2007.

———. *Blood of Abraham; Insights Into the Middle East.* Fayetteville, AR: University of Arkansas Press, 2007.

———. *Living Faith.* New York, NY: Random House, 1996.

———. *Our Endangered Values.* New York, NY: Simon & Schuster, 2005.

———. *Palestine: Peace Not Apartheid.* New York, NY: Simon & Schuster, 2007.

———. "Presidential Inaugural Address." Thursday, January 20, 1977. http://www.jimmycarterlibrary.org/documents/speeches/inaugadd. phtml (accessed April 22, 2010).

———. *Sources of Strength: Meditations on Scripture for a Living Faith.* New York, NY: Random House, 1997.

————. *Talking Peace: A Vision for the Next Generation.* Rev. ed. New York, NY: Puffin Books, 1995.

————. *The Virtues of Aging.* New York, NY: Random House, 1998.

————. *We Can Have Peace in the Holy Land.* New York, NY: Simon & Schuster, 2009.

Carter, Jimmy and Rosalynn Carter. *Everything to Gain: Making the Most out of the Rest of Your Life.* Fayetteville, AR: University of Arkansas Press, 1995.

Carter, Rosalynn. *Helping Someone with Mental Illness: A Compassionate Guide for Family, Friends, and Caregivers.* New York, NY: Three Rivers Press, 1999.

Carter, Rosalynn, Susan Golant, and Kathryn Cade. *Within Our Reach: Ending the Mental Health Crisis.* New York, NY: Rodale Press, 2010.

Center on Poverty and Inequality at Stanford University. "Twenty Facts About US Inequality that Everyone Should Know, CEO Pay." http://stanford.edu/group/scspi-dev/cgi-bin/fact2.php, fact9.php, fact10.php (accessed February 21, 2010).

Chen, Shaohua, and Martin Ravallion. "The Developing World Is Poorer than We Thought, but No Less Successful in the Fight Against Poverty." Development Research Group, World Bank. http://www-wds.worldbank.org/external/default/WDSContentServer/IW3P/IB/2010/01/21/000158349_20100121133109/Rendered/PDF/WPS4703.pdf (accessed June 9, 2010).

Children of the Night, Facebook page, http://www.facebook.com/home.php?ref=home#!/pages/Children-of-the-Night-Saving-Americas-Children-from-Prostitution/185199382500?ref=ts (accessed March 2, 2010).

Chrysostom, St. John. Homily 15 on St. Matthew: On the Beatitudes. Translated by Rev. Sir George Prevost, Bt., 1851. Revised American edition by Rev. Matthew B. Riddle, 1888. The St. Pachomius Orthodox Library, Nativity 1997. http://www.voskrese.info/spl/matthom15.html (accessed July 4, 2010).

Chrysostom, St. John. *On Wealth and Poverty.* Translated by Catharine P. Roth. Yonkers. NY: St. Vladimir's Seminary Press, 1981.

Coleman-Jensen, Alisha, Mark Nord, Margaret Andrews, and Steven Carlson. Household Food Security in the United States in 2010. ERR-125, U.S. Dept. of Agriculture, Econ. Res. Serv. September 2011, p5 & 14.

Collins, Jim. *Good to Great and the Social Sectors: A Monograph to Accompany Good to Great.* New York, NY: HarperCollins, 2005.

Colvin, Geoff. *Talent Is Overrated: What Really Separates World-Class Performers from Everybody Else.* New York, NY: Penguin Books, 2008.

Crosby, Michael H. *Spirituality of the Beatitudes: Matthew's Vision for the Church in an Unjust World.* Maryknoll, NY: Orbis Books, 2005.

Crutchfield, Leslie, and Heather McLeod Grant. *Forces for Good: The Six Practices of High-Impact Nonprofits.* San Francisco, CA: Jossey Bass, 2008.

CVP.ucsf.edu, "The Center for Vulnerable Populations at UCSF," http://cvp.ucsf.edu/ (accessed July 4, 2012).

Dalai Lama, The. *Ethics for the New Millennium.* New York, NY: Riverhead Books, 1999.

———, *An Open Heart, Practicing Compassion in Everyday Life.* New York, NY: Bay Back Books, 2002.

Daniel, Lillian. "Caution: Contents May be Hot (Matthew 5:1-12)." *The Christian Century.* 2002-01-16119:2, 16(1).

David, Rosalie. *Religion and Magic in Ancient Egypt.* New York, NY: Penguin Books. 2002.

Day, Dorothy. *Selected Writings.* Maryknoll, NY: Orbis Books, 2007.

Dear, John, SJ. *The God of Peace: Toward a Theology of Nonviolence.* Eugene, OR: Wipf & Stock, 2008.

————. *Living Peace: A Spirituality of Contemplation and Action.* New York, NY: Doubleday, 2004.

————. *A Persistent Peace; One Man's Struggle for a Nonviolent World.* Chicago, IL: Loyola Press, 2008.

————. *Jesus, the Rebel; Bearer of God's Peace and Justice.* Chicago, IL: Sheed and Ward, 2000.

————. *The Questions of Jesus: Challenging Ourselves to Discover Life's Great Answers.* New York, NY: Doubleday, 2004.

Dees, J. Gregory. *Strategic Tools for Social Entrepreneurs: Enhancing the Performance of Your Enterprising Nonprofit.* New York, NY: Wiley, 2002.

DeNavas-Walt, Carmen, Bernadette D. Proctor, and Jessica C. Smith. "Income, Poverty, and Health Insurance Coverage in the United States." *U.S. Census Bureau, Current Population Reports 2008.* Washington, DC: US Government Printing Office, 2009.

Dodds, Bill, and Michael Dodds. *Happily Ever After Begins Here and Now: Living the Beatitudes Today.* Loyola Press, 1997.

Ehrenreich, Barbara. *Nickled and Dimed: On (Not) Getting By in America.* New York, NY: Henry Holt & Company, 2002.

————. *Bright-sided: How the Relentless Promotion of Positive Thinking has Undermined America.* New York, NY: Metropolitan Books, 2009.

Elfenworks.org, "The Elfenworks Foundation" http://www.elfenworks. org/about (accessed December 30, 2011).

Elkington, John, and Pamela Hartigan. *The Power of Unreasonable People: How Social Entrepreneurs Create Markets That Change the World.* Boston: Harvard Business School Press, 2008.

Ellwood, Robert and Barbara McGraw. *Many Peoples, Many Faiths: Women and Men in the World Religions, Ninth Edition.* Upper Saddle River, NJ: Prentice Hall, 2009.

Errico, Rocco. *Setting a Trap for God: The Aramaic Prayer of Jesus*. Unity Village, MO: Unity House, 1975.

Epstein, Paul, Paul Coates, and Lyle Wray. *Results That Matter: Improving Communities by Engaging Citizens, Measuring Performance, and Getting Things Done*. San Francisco, CA: Jossey Bass, 2006.

Ferguson, George. Signs and Symbols in Christian Art. London: Oxford University Press, 1961.

Ferris, Marc. "Arianna Huffington Delivers Keynote Speech at Sarah Lawrence Commencement Ceremony." *New Rochelle Patch*. New Rochelle, NY: May, 2011. Online at http://newrochelle.patch.com/articles/arianna-huffington-delivers-keynote-speech-at-sarah-lawrence-commencement-ceremony (accessed June 26, 2012).

Forest, Jim. *The Ladder of the Beatitudes*. Maryknoll, NY: Orbis Books, 1999.

Gill, David. *Becoming Good: Building Moral Character*. Downers Grove, IL: Intervarsity Press, 2000.

———. *Doing Right: Practicing Ethical Principles*. Downers Grove, IL: Intervarsity Press, 2004.

Gills, James P. *Overcoming Spiritual Blindness*. Lake Mary, FL: Creation House, 2005.

Gordon, Nehemia. *The Hebrew Yeshua vs. the Greek Jesus*. Arlington, TX: Hilkiah Press, 2005.

Grace, Kay Sprinkel, and Alan Wendroff. *High Impact Philanthropy: How Donors, Boards, and Nonprofit Organizations Can Transform Communities*. New York, NY: John Wiley & Sons, 2001.

Gray, George Buchanan. *The Forms of Hebrew Poetry Considered with Special Reference to the Criticism and Interpretation of the Old Testament*, London: Hodder & Stoughton, 1915.

Greenleaf, Robert. *Servant Leadership: A Journey Into the Nature of Legitimate Power and Greatness*. Mahwah, NJ: Paulist Press, 1977.

Grusky, David, and Emily Ryo. "Did Katrina Recalibrate Attitudes toward Poverty and Inequality? A Test of the 'Dirty Little Secret' Hypothesis," *Du Bois Review: Social Science Research on Race* 3, no. 1 (Spring 2006), 59-82. http://katrinaresearchhub.ssrc.org/dubois-review-issue-katrina-unmasking-race-poverty-and-politics-in-the-21st-century/resource_view (accessed March 5, 2010).

Grusky, David and Szonja Szelényi, eds. *The Inequality Reader: Contemporary and Foundational Readings in Race, Class, and Gender.* Boulder, CO: Westview Press, 2006.

Guiness, Os. *The Call: Finding and Fulfilling the Central Purpose of Your Life.* Nashville, TN: Thomas Nelson Press, 1998.

Gundry, Robert. *Matthew, A Commentary on his Literary and Theological Art.* Grand Rapids, MI: Eerdmans Press, 1982.

Haggerty, Rosanne. *Ending Homelessness in South Australia.* South Australian Government - Department of the Premier & Cabinet, Adelaide Thinkers in Residence. Australia, July 2005, http://www.socialinclusion.sa.gov.au/files/Homelessness_Ending.pdf (accessed June 26, 2012).

Hall, Mitch. *Peace Quest: Cultivating Peace in a Violence Culture.* Sausalito, CA: Peace Quest, 2004.

Hakes, Jay. "Can Measuring Results Produce Results: One Manager's View." *Evaluation and Program Planning* 24 (2001): 319-327.

Hammond, Sue Annis. *The Thin Book of Appreciative Inquiry.* Bend, OR: ThinBook, 1996.

Hanh, Thich Nhat. *Being Peace.* Berkeley, CA: Parallax Press, 1987.

Harrelson, Walter J., ed. *New Interpreter's Study Bible: New Revised Standard Version with the Apocrypha.* Nashville, TN: Abingdon Press, 2003.

Harrington, Daniel. *Sacra Pagina; The Gospel of Matthew.* Collegeville, MN: Liturgical Press, 2007.

Hayes, John. S*ub-merge: Living Deep in a Shallow World: Service, Justice and Contemplation Among the World's Poor.* Ventura, CA: Regal Books, 2006.

Hebrew for Christians. "The Beatitudes of Jesus." http://www.hebrew-4christians.com/Scripture/Brit_Chadashah/Beatitudes/beatitudes. html (accessed March 15, 2010).

Henson, John. *Good as New, A Radical Retelling of the Scriptures.* Alresford, UK: John Hunt Publishing, 2004.

Hoffman, Erick. *The Wisdom of Maimonides: The Life and Writings of the Jewish Sage.* Boston, MA: Trumpeter Press, 2008.

Hopkins, Donald, M.D., "Carter Center Guinea Worm Eradication Effort Briefing" Port St. Lucie, FL: The Carter Center, February 24, 2010.

Hopkins, Donald. *The Greatest Killer, Smallpox in History.* Chicago, IL: Chicago University Press, 2002.

Howard, George. *Hebrew Gospel of Matthew.* Macon, GA: Mercer University Press, 1995.

Hubbard, Scott. *Exploring Mars.* Tuscon, AZ: University of Arizona Press, 2011.

Imhoff, Roland, and Rainer Banse. "Ongoing Victim Suffering Increases Prejudice: The Case of Secondary Anti-Semitism," *Psychological Science*, December 2009. Excerpted in "Social Justice: Long Suffering Falls Short," *Stanford Social Innovation Review* (Spring 2010).

Inequality.com, "The Center on Poverty and Inequality at Stanford University," http://www.inequality.com/ (accessed July 4, 2010).

Jacobs, Jane. *The Death and Life of Great American Cities.* New York, NY: Random House, 1961.

Johnston, David. "The Gap Between Rich and Poor Grows in the United States." *The New York Times* (March 29, 2007). http://www.nytimes.com/2007/03/29/business/worldbusiness/29iht-income.4.5075504.html (accessed June 24, 2012).

Keck, James (May 30, 2010). "Holy, Holy, Holy in the Year That King Uzziah Died; Sermon #876"*Sermons of First-Plymouth Congregational Church, UCC.* Lincoln, NE : First Plymouth Congregational Church. http://www.firstplymouth.org/sermons/10_sermons/05-30-10.pdf (accessed June 5, 2010).

Kragen, Ken. *Life is a Contact Sport: Ten Great Career Strategies That Work.* New York, NY: William Morrow, 1994.

Law, Anwi Skinses and Richard A. Wisniewski, *Kalaupapa National Historic Park and the Legacy of Father Damien, A Pictorial History.* Honolulu: Pacific Basin Enterprises, 2007, with stapled updated insert, 2010.

Lehmann, Heidi. "The War on Women and Girls." Momentum. http://www.momentumconference.org/speaker-presentation/speaker/heidi-lehmann/presentation/the-war-on-women-and-girls/index.html (accessed June 10, 2010).

Letts, Christine, William Ryan, and Allen Grossman. *High Performance Nonprofit Organizations: Managing Upstream for Greater Impact.* New York, NY: John Wiley & Sons, 1999.

Lewis, Stephen. "A Crisis of Gender Violence." Momentum. http://www.momentumconference.org/speaker-presentation/speaker/stephen-lewis/presentation/a-crisis-of-gender-violence/index.html (accessed June 10, 2010).

Lindberg, Tod. "What the Beatitudes Teach." *Policy Review*, September 2007. http://www.hoover.org/publications/policyreview/8810342.html (accessed April 19, 2010).

Lynch, Kevin, and Julius Walls. *Mission, Inc.: The Practitioner's Guide to Social Enterprise.* San Francisco, CA: Berrett-Koehler Publishers, 2009.

McDonald, Patricia M. *God and Violence: Biblical Resources for Living in a Small World.* Scottdale, PA: Herald Press, 2004.

McKinsey & Company, Inc., "Developing an Effective Management Organization: The Carter Center," Fellows and Senior Staff Retreat, December 11, 1992.

McLaren, Brian, Elisa Padilla, and Ashley Bunting Seeber, eds. *The Justice Project*. Grand Rapids, MI: Baker Books, 2009.

McReynolds, Paul, ed. *Word Study Greek-English New Testament, with Complete Concordance*. Carol Stream, IL: Tyndale House Publishers, 1990.

Meadors, Gary. "The 'Poor' in the Beatitudes of Matthew and Luke." *Grace Theological Journal* 6.2 (1985): 305-314.

Merton, Thomas. *The Pocket Thomas Merton*. Boston, MA: New Seeds Books, 2005.

Metaxas, Eric. *Dietrich Bonhoeffer: Pastor, Martyr, Prophet, Spy*. Nashville, TN: Thomas Nelson, 2010.

Metzger, Bruce and Michael Coogan, eds. *Oxford Guide to the Bible*. Oxford, New York, NY: Oxford University Press, 1993.

Miles, Steven. *The Hippocratic Oath and the Ethics of Medicine*. New York, NY: Oxford University Press, 2005.

Minear, Paul. "The Salt of the Earth." *Interpretation* (January 1997): 34.

Molnar, Michael. *The Star of Bethlehem: The Legacy of the Magi*. New Brunswick: Rutgers University Press, 2000.

Monk of St. Tikhon's Monastery, ed. *These Truths We Hold – The Holy Orthodox Church: Her Life and Teachings*. South Canaan, PA: St. Tikhon's Seminary Press, 1986.

Mounce, William, and Robert H. Mounce, eds. *The Zondervan Greek and English Interlinear New Testament (NASB/NIV)*. Grand Rapids, MI: Zondervan, 2008.

Moss, Ambler, Francis More and Samuel Lewis, "Carter Center Panama Canal Briefing," Port St. Lucie, FL, February 26, 2010.

Nicholls, Alex. *Social Entrepreneurship: New Models of Sustainable Social Change*. New York, NY: Oxford University Press, 2008.

Nonharming.com, "The Center for Non Harming Ministries," http://www.nonharming.com/ (accessed December 30, 2011).

Oleska, Michael. *Orthodox Alaska: A Theology of Mission.* St. Vladimir's Seminary Press. Crestwood, New York, NY: 1992.

Peck, Don. "How a New Jobless Era Will Transform America." *The Atlantic.* March 2010, http://www.theatlantic.com/magazine/archive/2010/03/how-a-new-jobless-era-will-transform-america/7919/ (accessed April 18, 2010).

Phillips, Gary. "Happy Are They: Living the Beatitudes in America." *The Christian Century.* (July 30, 1997). http://findarticles.com/p/articles/mi_m1058/is_n22_v114/ai_19677255/?tag=content;col1 (accessed June 10, 2010).

Phills, James. *Integrating Mission and Strategy for Nonprofit Organizations.* New York, NY: Oxford University Press, 2005.

Powell, Mark Allan. "Matthew's Beatitudes: Reversals and Rewards of the Kingdom." *The Catholic Biblical Quarterly* 58/3 (1996) 460-79.

Rank, Mark, and Thomas A. Hirschl. "Estimating the Risk of Food Stamp Use and Impoverishment During Childhood." *Archive of Pediatric and Adolescent Medicine* (2009): 994-999.

Rawls, John. *Justice as Fairness.* Boston, MA: Harvard University Press, 2001.

Sachs, Jeffrey. *The End of Poverty: Economic Possibilities for Our Time.* New York, NY: Penguin Books, 2005.
Saint Ignatius of Loyola, *Personal Writings.* New York, NY: Penguin Classics, 2004.

Salkin, Jeffrey. *Being God's Partner: How to Find the Hidden Link Between Spirituality and Your Work.* Woodstock, NY: Jewish Lights Publishing, 1994.

Saller, Richard. Speech, during *A Concert for Hope.* Film directed by Lauren Speeth (Burlingame, CA: Elfenworks Productions, HD-DVD release), low-resolution film online at www.inequality.com.

Salm, Luke, FSC. *The Work Is Yours; The Life of Saint John Baptist de La Salle.* Landover, MD: Christian Brothers Publications, 1996.

Sider, Ronald. *Just Generosity.* Grand Rapids, MI: Baker Books, 1999.

Sider, Ronald, John Perkins, Wayne Gordon, and F. Albert Tizon. *Linking Arms, Linking Lives.* Grand Rapids, MI: Baker Books. 2008.

Singer, Jhos. "Divine Paradox: Judaism 101" San Mateo, CA: Congregational Church of San Mateo. August 29, 2009.

Speeth, Lauren. *A Guide for Uncharted Territory; A Critical Analysis of Former President James Earl "Jimmy" Carter's Seven Pillar Methodology for Implementing Lasting, Measurable Change, As Set in Relation to Jesus' Teachings of the Beatitudes, as Conveyed in the Gospel of Matthew.* Seattle, WA: Bakke Graduate University (dissertation), 2011.

Speeth, Lauren. *Tracks of Hope: The Forgotten Story of America's Runaway Train and How We Can Change Its Course.* San Francisco, CA: Blurb, 2007.

Stearns, Richard. *The Hole in Our Gospel: What Does God Expect of Us? The Answer That Changed My Life and Might Just Change the World.* Nashville, TN: Thomas Nelson, 2009.

Stone, Bryan. *Compassionate Ministry.* Maryknoll, NY: Orbis Books, 1996.

Stortz, Martha. *Blessed to Follow: The Beatitudes as a Compass for Discipleship.* Minneapolis, MN: Augsburg Fortress Press, 2008.

Strobel, Lee. *The Case for Christ: A Journalist's Personal Investigation of the Evidence for Jesus.* DVD. Directed by Michael Eaton and Timothy Eaton. Los Angeles, CA: Lions Gate, 2007.

TerraChoice Environmental Marketing, Inc., "The Seven Sins of Greenwashing," http://sinsofgreenwashing.org/ (accessed February 21, 2010).

Trimm, James Scott. *B'Sorot Matti: The Good News According to Matthew from An Old Hebrew Manuscript.* Hurst, TX: Hebrew/Aramaic New Testament Research Institute, 1990.

Trzyna, Thomas. *Blessed Are the Pacifists: The Beatitudes and Just War Theory.* Scottdale, PA: Herald Press, 2006.

UHCAN.org, "The Universal Health Care Action Network," http://www.uhcan.org/ (accessed July 4, 2010).

UN Department of Economic and Social Affairs. "Rethinking Poverty; Report on the World Social Situation 2010." New York, NY: 2009. Under "Preface," http://www.un.org/esa/socdev/rwss/docs/2010/fullreport.pdf (accessed June 10, 2010).

Van Kasteren, John Peter. "The Eight Beatitudes." *The Catholic Encyclopedia.* Vol. 2. New York, NY: Robert Appleton Company, 1907. http://www.newadvent.org/cathen/02371a.htm (accessed February 22, 2010).

Van Til, Kent. *Less than Two Dollars a Day; a Christian View of World Poverty and the Free Market.* Grand Rapids, MI: Eerdmans Publishing, 2007.

Welch, Wilford. *Tactics of Hope: How Social Entrepreneurs Are Changing Our World.* San Rafael, CA: Earth Aware Editions, 2008.

Western, Bruce. *Punishment and Inequality in America.* New York, NY: Russell Sage Foundation, 2006.

Weston, Anthony. *A 21st Century Ethical Toolbox.* New York, NY: Oxford University Press, 2001.

White, Randy. *Journey to the Center of the City; Making a Difference in an Urban Neighborhood.* Downers Grove, IL: Intervarsity Press, 1996.

Williams, Roy. *God, Actually: Why God Probably Exists, Why Jesus Was Probably Divine, and Why the "Rational" Objections to Religion are Unconvincing.* Oxford, UK: Lion, 2009.

Wilson, William Julius. *More than Just Race: Being Black and Poor in the Inner City (Issues of our Time).* New York, NY: W.W. Norton & Co., 2010.

Winkler, Gershon. *The Way of the Boundary Crosser, An Introduction to Jewish Flexidoxy*. Northvale, NJ: Jason Aronson, 1998.

Wolk, Andrew, and Kelley Kreitz. *Business Planning for Enduring Social Impact: A Social-Entrepreneurial Approach to Solving Social Problems*. Cambridge, MA: Root Cause Publishing, 2008.

Young, Andrew. *The Carpenter's Apprentice: A Spiritual Biography of Jimmy Carter*. Grand Rapids, MI: Zondervan Books, 1996.

youTube.com/elfenworks, "The Elfenworks' YouTube Channel," http://www.youTube.com/elfenworks (accessed July 4, 2010).

Young, Rowena. "For What It Is Worth: Social Value and the Future of Social Entrepreneurship." *Social Entrepreneurship: New Models of Sustainable Social Change*, ed. Alex Nicholls (New York, NY: Oxford University Press, 2008), 61.

Zander, Rosamund Stone and Benjamin Zander. *The Art of Possibility: Transforming the Professional and Personal.* Boston: Harvard Business School Press, 2000.

SEARCH INDEX

"Is there a distinctively American approach to taking on poverty and other social problems? Indeed there is: We've long been skeptical of government solutions and have looked to philanthropy and social entrepreneurship as a main line of defense against social problems of all kinds. If social entrepreneurship is the grand American bet, then much rests on ensuring that our bet pays off. We need a book that tells us what works, what doesn't work, and what can be done to ensure that entrepreneurship delivers on its grand promise. This is precisely that book."

**– DAVID B. GRUSKY, DIRECTOR,
STANFORD CENTER ON POVERTY AND INEQUALITY**

"Poverty is America's elephant in the drawing room. Dr. Speeth's book is that of a most rare species of philanthropic activists, one who approaches a seemingly monolithic and intractable reality, with compassion and generosity of spirit, yes, but most importantly, with entrepreneurial innovation and a concrete, action-by-action road map for transformative change."

**– DRUCILLA RAMEY, ESQ., DEAN,
GOLDEN GATE UNIVERSITY SCHOOL OF LAW**

"As a social entrepreneur and the CEO of an impact investment company, these seven pillars resonate with the daily challenges that we face. The right balance of social impact and commercial sustainability is comparable to riding a bike, and the seven pillars will help keep you moving forward to maintain balance and momentum. I would recommend that anyone considering investing in a social entrepreneur should incorporate these seven pillars into their due diligence process."

– GIL CRAWFORD, CEO, MICROVEST CAPITAL FUNDS

"A helpful and realistic guide to social entrepreneurship by a caring and committed practitioner."

**– PHIL WISE, VICE PRESIDENT OF OPERATIONS,
THE CARTER CENTER**